Angels On Our Side

This book is dedicated to the memory of
Diana Marjorie Alborough
1931 - 2017

Welcome to Dominic and Alison's World

'Angels On Our Side' is Dominic and Alison's most comprehensive book to date. From his young beginnings as a four year old boy, laying in his bed, scared stiff hardly daring to move. His 'growing up' years, practical jokes and his time working aboard Radio Caroline; to his current psychic adventures alongside his wife Alison.

Ghost hunting in Wales, alien spotting in London, England, and running around the Norfolk countryside chasing lost animals.

Destiny Television   how Dominic got to present his own Psychic show on SKY Television.

The story behind Dominic's friendship with George Michael, helping the internationally acclaimed song writer come to terms with his own faith.

Stories of mediumship which will make you laugh and cry, all in the same paragraph. Alongside Dominic's teachings and philosophies. How to read an aura, plus meet your Spirit Guides and Mentors, plus open up your first sense –'Intuition'.

As Dominic says "Little miracles happen every day."

www.myndsite.org

DOMINIC ZENDEN

Dominic J Zenden lives in North Norfolk with his wife Alison.

Dominic devotes the majority of his time to his main passion in life, the paranormal. Now in his mid-fifties he is referred to as an expert in this subject and writes for 'Spirit' and 'Destiny' magazine on anything considered to be out of the ordinary.

Dominic works as a 'Spirit Medium', 'Aura Reader' (profiling personalities from photographs.) And a 'Past Lives regression' and 'Future Lives' progression therapist. As well as holding a very keen interest in Extra-terrestrial Life.

Dominic's hobbies are painting, (his Angel Art sells all over the World.) Sport, (a life-long football fan.)

Dominic has a degree in Psychology and enjoys helping people understand the dynamics of adult relationships. His published book on self-help 'Coffee Cup Chatter' explains how he believes better relationships can be formed by having a clearer understanding of how people think and act.

Angels On Our Side is Dominic's most comprehensive book on his beliefs, philosophies, teachings and experiences.

Other books (to date) published by Dominic:

Spirit Motivator - 2006

Naught or Thought - 2014

Coffee Cup Chatter - 2015

Aura – Life in 4D - 2015

The Little Christmas Tree - 2015

My Childhood Room - 2016

FOREWORD

I am honoured to be asked to write this foreword for Dominic Zenden's book, 'Angels On Our Side'. Within each chapter Dominic looks at his own life and development spiritually, with fascinating stories which will be of great interest to the reader. This book also gives great information for the reader to look at and understand areas such as mediumship, meditation, past lives, etc., to mention just a few. What I particularly like is that it's a book you can read from cover to cover, yet return to it time and time again to dip into various chapters; which will interest you and help you think about your own life's progress. It is very well written, inspirational and highly recommended.

Rev Philip Solomon, BA Hons., IWO Dip.

Introduction to Mediumship and The Afterlife by my friend and mentor Philip Solomon

So many times I have been asked the question, "What is the Spirit World like?" Most information about what it is has been received through spiritual messages. There can be no other way for us to have this knowledge; and modern Spiritualism has focused on offering proof of the life hereafter.

I often think it is incorrect to believe Spiritualism only started in 1848 with Hydesville in America, and then spread throughout the world after the First World War, when so many people were desperate to know their loved ones carried on in a higher life. I believe that the practices of sensitives being able to facilitate messages between the two worlds probably goes back to the very earliest days of human habitation of the world as we know it.

The Spirit World operates at a faster and higher rate of vibration than that which is experienced by those of us on the Earth Plane. Mediums and sensitives have to learn to quicken their vibration to get close enough to receive snippets of wisdom and messages of love and light from the 'Other Side'.

It must also be remembered that the Spirit World has many levels of consciousness. There are those who will say that mediums are born and it is true that there are some who do arrive in this world with such gifts. However, I believe that with training and the proper lifestyle application, everyone can develop mediumistically.

I also take the view that a knowledge of mediumship and the afterlife is there for us while we sleep, and that sometimes our spirit, (we are all spirit energy, by the way) visits the higher realms and is sampled through our dreams. Of course these dreams may be painted by our daily experiences and things that have pleased us and, indeed, scared us, but at other times I think we are given the experience of a wonderful visit to the higher life, and perhaps meeting or seeing our loved ones who have recently or distantly passed. Our pets can be there as well, for these animals and creatures that have lived with us in the physical life go to the higher life and level, where the humans they loved abound.

Spirit life is not that different to our Earthly life really, except that we do not have to work, pay the bills, and suffer pain and illness, and whatever you would really wish to do can quite easily be within your reach in the higher life. When we first pass over, what drives us on the Earth plane will probably also drive us in the spiritual realm, but eventually progression will take place which is part of the journey of each and every one of us, in this life and the next.

Philip Solomon

Contents

Inspiration

It's 8.20am, Saturday 13th October 2018. Dominic and I are discussing 'spiritual' occurrences which have happened to us.

Suddenly, without warning I see (on our lounge carpet) a large, floaty colourful angel, rising up slowly towards the ceiling; purple in the centre, edged by a deep, dark blue.

The angel floated along the ceiling, almost like a splodge of vibrant paint, then disappeared out of the window.

As the angel left another emerged from the same place on the carpet, repeating exactly the same pattern. It rose upwards, same colours, travelled along the ceiling, then through the window.

Mesmerised I sat there, staring at 'angel after angel' floating upwards in front of me.

A couple of these 'swirling angels' had the face of old men, not peering at me, just appearing there. They too, glided upwards, then sideways before leaving us.

Around ten to fifteen continued, one after the other, lighting up the moment.

I was transfixed, explaining to Dominic exactly what I was experiencing; as I had never seen such beautiful angelic energies.

That 'moment' shouted out at us, and we felt this was of such significance we should name the book we are writing 'Angels On Our Side'.

The Angels on the cover (front and back) are drawn by Dominic; and I too saw these angels at 8.20am, Saturday 13th October 2018.

Alison Zenden.

INTRODUCTION

I first heard Dominic in 2009 when he was a 'guest speaker' on local radio. Dominic was speaking about his first published book 'Spirit Motivator', alongside doing 'live mediumship' for listeners phoning into the radio station.

This 'phone in' proved very successful and I intended to make an appointment to have a reading myself.

A few weeks later I knocked on the white door of a modern block of flats and a very friendly approachable face greeted me.
The atmosphere immediately felt warm and very comfortable.
On the walls were various spiritual pictures including unique brightly coloured angels which I later discovered Dominic had painted himself.
This was an idyllic setting for the next hour of mediumship where a good connection was made.

I became very interested in Dominic's work including the other areas 'past life regression' etc. Dominic has been a past life regression therapist for over 30 years with hundreds of clients experiencing this through hypnotherapy.

Dominic teaches psychic development and holds classes throughout the world.

With a vast knowledge and a deep passion for what he believes in Dominic helps people from all walks of life, including celebrities and royalty.

Over the last few decades he has become a very reputable and recognised medium.

This book details Dominic's psychic skills and a combination of personal experiences and detailed psychic stories, all borne during a time where the word 'psychic' wasn't as acceptable as it is today.

'Angels On Our Side' is the sixth book Dominic has written alongside contributions from myself.

We hope you enjoy the collection.

Alison Zenden

The Corridor of Life

As we walk 'The Corridor of Life'
There's love, laughter, doom and strife.
Plan your route to open doors,
Many feet tread on these floors.
Depending on the rooms we choose
Our memories we will never lose.
Walk in 'the now', live for today
Laughter's infectious, so give some away.
Kind words, touch, share a smile
Make others special, for a short while.

As one door closes in 'The Laughter Room'
We may enter another 'Full of Gloom'.
Make your entrance, words softly spoken
Grief is felt, people broken.

The corridors are not always a 'bed of roses'
Many 'if's and but's', not sweet reposes.
We march ahead, venture through
The universe is here for you.
The 'Room of Love' we all wish to find
Keep marching forward, don't look behind
And as we walk this Earthly plane
Some 'Pass on', and 'some remain'.
It's called 'The Corridor of Life'
You may have met a husband or wife.
We're all human beings, have stories to tell
Hope you've walked yours very well
As the final door opens and life's at an end
The room in my hearts' always open my friend.

Alison Zenden

CHAPTER ONE

The Early Days

I love life, a simple but true statement.

Even in the darkest deepest moments of uncertainty I still love life.

Where else could you experience the wonders of a sunset? Or the clouds across the moon? The taste of strawberries? The cold morning air on a December day?

I believe life is for living. The experiences we have whilst in a mortal body are the memories that we get to keep for eternity.

I have never believed death is the end, how could I? Ever since I was young enough to think I have had voices in my head. Not my voice, but the voices of those who have moved on to the realm of spirit.

For a child it was normal just to accept without question or thought. The voices were real, so the logical way to think is that everyone hears the same. Until one night.

Voices

I was laying in my bed, covers and quilt pulled tight up against my face. Everything in the house was still. I could hear the clock tick from the living room, just down the hallway from my ground floor bedroom. Never heard it during the day, but at night time that small wooden clock sounded as loud as a horse trotting down the hallway. I lay transfixed, hardly daring to move as the sound of footsteps came into my room from outside. Someone must be outside my bedroom window?

By now fear had gripped me, as the footsteps came again, only closer this time, right outside my bedroom window.

Then without warning a friendly grey-haired man came into mind sight, his face old; his voice warm and friendly.

Smiling, he calmed me down, the smooth voice reassuring in its gentleness.

This spirit voice and image was my Grandfather George (my mother's father who had crossed over to the realm of spirit just after I was born.) I was told later that he had been gassed during the Second World War and had never recovered; finally submitting to pulmonary disease in his early seventies.

A brave man like many of his generation.

After his voice and kind words I fell back to sleep, not waking until I heard the heavy footsteps of my father trudging down the stairs. His daily routine starting with his normal coughing fit whilst he drew on his cigarette. The toxic aroma would fill my room, as it travelled at the speed of light from his chair in the living room down the hall and right under my nose. I truly hated that smell.

Do not tell Lies

Over breakfast, I told my mother that George, her father, had helped me the previous night. At first my mother listened with just one ear, making sandwiches for my elder brother's packed lunch for school.

I continued, "Grandad George was very kind" I said, without warning, she stopped buttering the bread and came right up close to me so she did not have to shout, and said "do not tell lies" - giving me a look that would sour cream. I took it she was not interested. After all I knew what had happened, but this was the first time that I had the realisation that not everyone heard and saw people in their minds eye.

From that point onwards my young life became more complicated.

Manners Please

I never spoke out loud about what was going on inside my mind. No point, my parents did not see what I did. From their perspective I can look back and see how difficult it was to understand a little boy who had his own ideas about life. I am sure looking back they must have thought I was attention seeking. Being the middle child of three was not a good place to be born. My elder brother (four years senior) and my sister (two years junior.) I was caught in the middle with not much going for me when it came to attention. I can recall both my parents being distant and cold. No hugs, or kisses; just left to get on with playing in my bedroom. Even meal times were an obstacle course of navigating the rules and conditions of eating.

My father was extremely strict. He would bark instructions across the table. We all had to eat everything on our plates, and if we were to speak whilst eating, we would find ourselves in deep trouble. Deep trouble would normally mean being beaten. His belt and my mother's wooden spoon would become objects of fear for all four of us.

I came to dislike meal times, even now I feel compelled to eat everything on my plate fifty years later.

Katie

By now I had started going to school. The journey was a two mile bus trip, I was nearly six years old. My birthday fell in September which meant I had just missed the cut off point by two weeks for the previous school year. I was one of the eldest in my year, which did give me an advantage of being stronger and bigger than many of my class mates.

My first friend was a girl called Katie. We lived close and began a friendship, traveling to school together.

The bus would collect us both from the bottom of our road, and drop us back at the same spot. I never thought anything about this. It became routine to catch the bus with Katie each day. The bus fare was a small amount of pennies, but we soon found out that we could pay the driver one penny less and he would drop us both half a mile from home right next door to a tiny sweetshop. The penny would then be used to buy sweets which we would eat on the half a mile walk home.

Even at six I could figure out that what my parents did not know would not hurt them.

Yes, we had to cross a busy road by ourselves but the risk was worth the reward.

Days

Some days just stay with you always. I can remember the blue summer sky, not a cloud to be seen, Katie was fun to be around. We would dare each other to do stupid things, for a girl she was great company, so unlike my younger sister who was in truth a pest.

This day started in the same way, catching the bus to school. I can remember it was the run up to sports day. A day that we all looked forward too. I was bigger and stronger than most in my year, I would win, and I loved winning anything. The school would award ribbons, different colours for first, second and third. I would pin them on my tee shirt with pride.

We did our normally thing, gave the bus driver just enough to drop us both off outside the sweetshop.

I can remember going in buying my sweets and leaving Katie. Girls being girls took ages to choose, so I left her and waited outside.

I can still see this today, I watched as Katie stepped out of the shop and without giving it a second thought stepped straight into the road, not looking both ways. It was like watching my friend sleep walk right into a truck in slow-motion. No sound, just vivid colour.

I stood transfixed to the spot, and I watched as Katie's soul left her body, a bright shining light of pure energy.

Now you would think this was not a time to celebrate, but all I wanted to do was punch the air, jump for joy. My friend had left this world, a life completed. I could not be sad, though over the coming months and years I did miss her. She would still talk to me, in my mind I would see her smiling, hear her chatting, daring me to do something outrageous.

I can now look back still with tears of joy and sadness. In some moments I must confess I wonder what would have happened if I had stayed with her that late summer afternoon. (I still talk with her even now, years later. I believe it is Katie that keeps me young, connected to my inner child as I grow grey.)

Flying Colours

The next few weeks were lost in the haze of all the consequences. I had started to understand it was futile talking with adults about my voices, but now I had something else to worry about. My vision was changing, I could not look at an object, animal or person without seeing a wash of colours. The patterns would jump and swirl, mixing together then darting off in all directions. Voices would come at me, hostile voices of my parents and teachers like knives being speared in my direction, red and black. Gentle voices floating 'cloud like' towards me, yellow and light blue. Every single living thing, object and sound had its own colour signature.

I realised later in life these colours where the vibrations made by sound and heat. The aura, or the energy field that surrounds everything.

Over the years I learnt to understand the meanings behind the colours, different combinations denoting different meanings. I can sit for hours just watching the colours dance around a tree, changing with the seasons as they fade in winter and then light up again in the spring. I feel privileged to be able to witness such kaleidoscopic visions.

Back in my younger days my parents thought I was ill. I would hear them talking about me and my behaviour.

At the age of eight I was taken to the doctor, then to hospital and finally to the psychiatrists.

I went through tests on eyes, brain scans and what seemed like hours of questioning. I believe my parents felt the events with Katie had thrown me into a form of mental illness. The colours were my way of masking grief and gain attention. They could not have been more wrong. I had no grief, Katie was still with me. I found it difficult at such a young age to understand how adults thought. Such closed arrogant thinking, believing they were right no matter what. At no stage did my parents ever take the time to ask me about my colours or my voices.

When the hospital came back reporting that nothing was mentally wrong with me, my parents left me alone. I would never share anything with them, my world would be a secret place that I could explore or ignore, but rarely share.

As a child I would love taking risks, climbing the highest trees, jumping off swings at the highest point. Danger was not part of my own personal world.

Passions

I had two other passions, football and practical jokes.

Hours kicking a ball against a wall, or playing football with anyone who would be available.

My love of Arsenal Football Club started at around this time. I would have been about eight years old. No television in those early days, I would listen to the matches on my small blue transistor radio, the commentator's voices would burst into my ear through a small white plug-in ear piece. My senses would come alive as I smelt the grass and the mud being kicked up, mixed together with the toxic smell of cigarette smoke from the crowd.

In this world of radio I could escape from the colours and voices that would be a constant in my head. (I am still never far away from a radio forty-eight years on.)

Practical jokes were my other form of amusement. No one was safe, I would have been a nightmare child for any unsuspecting adult. Mustard sweets, black eye soap, hand buzzers, sneezing powder, etc. would all be stuffed into my pockets just waiting for a victim.

My main victim was my father.

He was born on the 9th May 1930. The eldest of three children. A piano tuner father and a mother who earned money writing. As there was little call for pianos to be tuned during the depression and then the war, it was my dad's mother who brought home the bacon, bread and even the odd 'cream cake'. (A story for another time!)

My father was the type of man who you felt 'safe' and 'afraid of' all at the same time.

Five foot seven inches with a commanding voice which had been honed during his time as a drill instructor with The Royal Air Force.

For my younger self he was fierce. Upset him at your peril. I would lay in my bottom bunk at night time dreaming up ways to get back at him. I must have been a child that every parent dreads. Knowing that I could not match or disobey him seemed to drive me on even more.

My father (like most people who were born in the 1930's) liked to smoke.

He would tell the story of being given a packet of cigarettes and a lighter for his fourteenth birthday in 1944. Cigarettes were not cheap during the war and his parents had little or no money. Such a gift was rare. He had been a smoker ever since. He smoked at every opportunity, in the car, whilst watching television, even in the toilet. I hated the smell of that acrid cigarette smoke.

As I lay in bed with the eiderdown quilt wrapped tight to my shoulders, facing the cold garage wall, unknown to my father I was hatching a plan. A plan that might if executed with expert timing, (just might) put him off smoking for the rest of his life.

Boom Bang a Bang.

It was the dead of night. I lay awake thinking of what I had to do. If I got this right it may change all of our lives.

The previous day I had brought with my pocket money (10 pence) a small packet of cigarette crackers.

I had found this tiny shop tucked away up a long street in my home town. It sold every type of practical joke you could imagine, squirting flowers, black face soap, nails through fingers and so on.

I was to become a regular visitor over the next few years.

The shop itself was crammed full, overflowing with slightly faded packets and dark corners. An old fashioned till stood upon a glass topped counter.

A man in a brown overall guarded it with one arm, seemingly wrapped around the top of the machine.

Laid under the glass flip top lid were small white packets with a comically drawn face of a man with an exploded cigarette in his mouth. His face black and puzzled, the remains of a once long and slender cigarette now flat. I wanted them right that moment.

The packet contained what I may only describe as little triangular pieces of cardboard, no bigger than a babies thumb nail.

The instructions read, 'Push into the end of cigarette'. Then in large letters 'ONLY ONE PER CIGARETTE' Of course I was going to completely ignore the last instruction!

My father was a man of routine. In bed most nights by 11 O'clock, up for work around at 7 am. Each morning I would hear the same thing. The sound of heavy footsteps from upstairs, the loud rather musical sound of him passing wind with every third step of the staircase, the sound of him pulling his chair out next to the table, the fumbling for his packet of cigarettes, not looking just tapping around the table until his hand came across the familiar feel of the cold metal of the lighter placed directly on top of the packet. Half dazed still, the rattle of the silver paper, then finally the 'click, click' of the lighter before he drew his first long deep intake. The tip of the cigarette would glow brightly for a moment, closely followed by a long coughing fit, which went on and on, before he would settle back down again.

It was the same routine each and every day. I would even smell that scent of smoke come wafting into my room, under my quilt and right up my nose.

This day was going to be different, the night before I had pre-loaded the front three cigarettes not just with one cracker, but four!
I thought such a little object could not do too much damage by itself. I had carefully replaced the foul smelling objects back into the packet, making sure to place the box with the lighter back in the exact same position. I then fell asleep, only waking when my father was already accompanying himself down the stairs with his usual tune. My heart was racing fast, 1 heard the chair being pulled out, the familiar sound of his hand reaching, the 'click, click' as the lighter failed to light the first two times, then the sharp drawing in of breath and before he could cough, the largest bang that you could of imagined!

By this time I was just peering round the partly open wooden door, hardly daring to look.

I saw my father's blackened face, cigarette in tatters, just the filter left intact between his tremoring lips, patting himself down to make sure he still had all his limbs!

My father's face was just like the one drawn on the packet, dazed and bewildered.

I was not going to hang around, I ran back to my bedroom, pulled my quilt right up over my face.

Like I said I must have been a nightmare of a child.

In my defence I had little in common with either of my parents, what else could I do? I was a child struggling for attention.

Senses

We 'sense' long before anything else, just in this world of 'do it now' and instant access. We have lost the ability to listen to our soul.
If 'Past Life' theory is right, and we have all been alive many times, the chances are we are re-living a life which we have rehearsed many times.
We have lived through the decisions, made the mistakes and suffered the consequences. All this information is stored in our soul. All we have to do is listen and allow our minds to accept the answers, even if we do not like what we are sensing.
To me the better we get at making choices, the better life becomes, the more we achieve.
If slowing down, inner calmness helps us understand the challenges of the moment ahead, then we should all consider allowing our souls to direct us.

Nothing Matters

There is nothing that matters. Yes we all get upset, and yes it passes. This time of year is all about 'new beginnings'. Time to let go and start again. The Autumn Solstice is this weekend. The end of summer and the bridge between light and dark. Preparation is done for the long dark days. This is the time 'to do'. Write down all of your negative thoughts, things you may have had difficulty with, and burn them. I am advised this is the moment. If I believe nothing matters, these two things combined will see me into the New Year. Every day something new comes up, a reaction, a problem, a deed that lightens my heart. All I wish for is the understanding to cope with each new situation as it arrives. As for autumn, cannot wait.

CHAPTER TWO

Moving On

My childhood life was horrid. I was not a nice child. Secretive, rude and ill behaved. I did not want to do anything I was told. Constant conflicts with my parents and siblings. I was just not that nice.

My years between eight and eighteen were to say the least difficult.

When I was ten my father was diagnosed with Muscular Sclerosis, a disease that eats away at the nervous system leaving the person unable to function. A slow death with no dignity. My father (a stubborn bully of a man) took ten years, from diagnosis to death. In my early life I knew nothing but illness and temper from him.

Looking back I am not surprised he found living such a struggle. My mother was little help, emotionally inept, with little intelligence or common sense.

My elder brother ran away from home at sixteen moving as far away as possible. This one act of self-protection affected me more than anything else in my teenage years. My sister was also little help, marrying at sixteen to escape any responsibility. I was left to handle my mother's emotional outbursts and my father's illness.

I was nineteen when my father died on 21 December 1981 at 6.20pm. He had been in a bad way for many months, so it was a relief when he made the short journey across to the realm of spirit.

He knew my beliefs, and would argue passionately that when you're dead your dead. He even went so far as telling me he wanted his ashes scattering on a windy day, so he could get up as many peoples noses as possible.

You can imagine my surprise when the same night as he left he came back through to me to say that he was wrong! He had never admitted to being wrong ever, not once whilst alive. I had always looked at him as a totally closed mind. No room for debate or discussion.

The sequence of events went like this, my father's death in December. My father's funeral just before the New Year. My mother met a new man in April, he moved in, in May. They got married in July, I was told to get out of my childhood house in September. I was just twenty.

My mother held no regard for me, or the help I had given her, the time spent doing so much for my father. I was out on my own. Her own selfish needs came before anything.

In the later years I have come to realise that she feared being left alone.

Cathy

The advert read, "Small room to rent in shared house." Just what I was looking for.

I could not afford much, even though my father had died the previous year, my mother had not shared out the money from my late father. (I found out later that he had left a large sum, plus pensions and the house mortgage free, to my knowledge none of the children ever received a penny from my father's estate.)

My wage of seventy pounds a week for rent, food and travel had to stretch.

I rang the number on the advert, a lady in her sixties with a strong Lancashire accent answered. "Yes the room is still available" It was about seven miles from home, a short bus journey. But I was keen to see it, after all, so I arranged to call round.

The house stood proud in the middle of the road, houses either side, semi-detached, bay windows, short driveway leading into a wooden fronted garage.

My heart was pounding as I lifted the heavy brass door knocker. The light through the front door window slowly darkened as the lady (who I would come to know as 'Cathy') approached and opened the front door. Her warm smile and friendly nature disguising the tired frown I felt from her.

Cathy was lovely, warm, friendly and very much alone. The house was not hers, but belonged to a friend who had let her live there for the rest of her life. She showed me up the stairs to what I can only describe as a modest box room. Just enough space to put a small single bed, a television and hang a few clothes. Not much, but I could afford it.

I would take it, at least I thought I was welcome, unlike home.

I had nothing very much, no car to transport my belongings, just a couple of suitcases which I had packed. All my childhood toys, games, schoolbooks, sporting trophies I left. Just no room. My mother was kind enough to throw all these personal items away without a second thought. Twenty years of memories gone in a single yellow skip.

So my life began at Elizabeth Avenue.

Cathy was a saint. So kind, understanding and caring. She was the one shining light. My life was tough. Cathy would often cook, wash and iron for me, and in turn I would keep the large rear garden tidy.

Hours of conversations about everything. She knew what I was, even though she had her own independent opinions on 'life after life'.

Her house was not haunted, it was just safe, and for the first time in my life I felt a part of someone else's world.

Elizabeth Avenue

I was to stay with Cathy for a year. I believe it took me that long to get over the trauma of the previous few years.

I was already figuring out that 'The Realm of Spirit' worked in ways that were more than coincidence.

Finding Cathy's house had been a massive stroke of luck. I could have finished up anywhere. I had no idea what lay in wait for me the day I picked up the local paper and read Cathy's advertisement.

To this day I believe that 'Spirit' look after me. Not all the time, but when I decide to acknowledge and work hand in hand with my guides, angels and mentors, I certainly sense them close.

If I turn my back on 'Spirit' nothing goes to plan, I find hurdles where none should be and life becomes complicated.

I am sure many of you would have discovered the exact same.

Church

I am not one for going to church; too many boring school assemblies knocked the need for any religious worship right out of me. I wanted to explore religion, understand the truth from the myth. Not have religious teachings imposed upon me without the right to question.

Just behind Elizabeth Avenue, about a ten minute walk away I discovered the 'Spiritual church'. A small building with not much going on out front, you could easily miss it, just walk on past, never stopping to read the small dark blue notice board screwed onto the brick wall just alongside a blue four paneled rather small front door. Behind the door was a little entrance hall, and this massive, fully fitted church, with speaker's platform, pulpit and font.

The atmosphere was friendly. I sensed that I would be spending much of my free time here.

I met a few of the regulars. Mary who made the tea and looked after the visiting mediums and speakers. Sally who ran the books! Then there was John. He did everything from the twice weekly healing sessions to changing the washer on a tap, or replacing the light bulbs. John soon became more like a father to me.

In the space of a few months I was starting to rebuild my life. Cathy who was more of a mother to me than my own, and John a wise man who was there to guide me through some of the more difficult choices.

From this point onwards they were my family, and still are today.

Mediums

In eight months I was able to watch some of the very best mediums when they visited the Spiritualist church. A big part of my education was learning from how they chose to talk to an audience. Some would stand bolt upright, not moving just turning their heads in the direction of the person they wanted to speak with. Then there were the mediums that need confirmation. The message had to be accepted before they could move on to the next person.

I discovered that mediums come from all different backgrounds, cultures and education.

As a young man I would watch intensely, picking out the best way for myself to pass over the evidence for survival.

One medium that stood out head and shoulders above all the others was a lady in her late seventies. Slim grey hair, smartly dressed in a blue trouser suit and white blouse. Kind smile, calm manner.

I can recall her being charismatic, some people just have that aura of friendliness about them.

That evening hardly anyone turned up, the rows of chairs were empty, a few people sat together in small groups. This medium then stood up and said a simple prayer, nothing more than about thirty seconds. This had the effect of stopping the low hum of conversation, chairs moved noisily back to face the front of the stage.

Then something unexpected happened. This lady walked down the side of the stage and started walking up and down between the rows of empty chairs. She spoke first in Chinese, then French and finally English. Holding conversations with her spirit guides, this lady was amazing, the few people watching starred transfixed, hardly daring to blink. Expressions blank.

She walked up and down, talking louder and louder, words that had no meaning echoed around the room in her unfamiliar words. As the volume increased and her voice grew stronger. The old grey lady was no more.

The next twenty minutes was taken up by this medium talking directly with each and every person in turn. Each received a message that was personal, clear and delivered in around twenty seconds. Her voice would change as her language switched from Chinese to French and then English.

This was the best I had ever seen, a true demonstration of 'spirit contact'. No fanfares, or big speeches, just pure mediumship.

This one medium had showed me what I needed to know. She was the one that set the standard that every other medium should follow.

No questions, no personal comment, or "do you understand", just evidence of life after life.

Even to this day, years later I remember the impact this one medium had. I do my best to copy her, not in the language but in her delivery. Short messages, so everyone can have their own individual proof. I believe that when you come to see me work everyone in the audience has a message waiting. It is just down to my skill and work rate whether or not those 'letters' from your loved ones get passed on. One thing I can promise is that I try so very hard to make that happen. I may not be the same standard as this lady medium but I will always strive to reach her level.

Radio Caroline

I never wanted to say goodbye to Cathy or John, they were incredible people. I also loved the church, but I knew that if I was ever going to explore the world it had to be now. I was nearly twenty one and ready to go. If my father's passing had taught me anything it was to make the most of every day.

I had decided to join The Royal Air Force. I passed all the written exams, and the medical but had six months before I could sign.

So what does a young man with six months free do with that time? Well I ran away again, this time to sea to work on 'Radio Caroline'. Yes it was broadcasting illegally from the North Sea, yes I was taking a risk. If I had been caught on my way out, or my way back it would have meant prosecution, and a criminal record. This in turn would have put my ambitions to join the forces at risk. But I was fully aware of the consequences. I also knew that this may be my only chance to work in radio. After all it was not the type of career I had ever thought would be possible.

So here I was, back pack on, warm knitted hat (a gift from Cathy) and a stack of some of my favourite vinyl tucked neatly away in a Sainsbury's bag, waiting to board the 'fishing boat come supply ship' which would make the trip across from the east coast to international waters. If this was show business it was not very glamourous.

The trip across the sea was a nightmare. The boat did not go straight, it went right and left, zig- zagging across the North Sea. The smell of diesel coupled with the rocking of the waves brought on bouts of sickness which the crew found so very amusing. It took four hours of stomach churning, foul smelling claustrophobia inducing, wave battering time to reach the bright red hull of 'Radio Caroline.'

This was however just the beginnings of the danger!

The sea was not still, waves as big as our boat tossed us up, then down, back then forward. The crew threw a rope up and across, and I thought great they are going to winch us up and across. How wrong I was! The rope was for supplies, bags of rice, potatoes, meat and vegetables, all pulled along and then over onto the deck of the radio station.

I was hoping it wasn't so, but it was. To get on board you had to make a jump for it! Imagine the picture. I'm stood on deck, soaking wet, the wind rapping round my legs, red woolly hat, back pack, Sainsbury's bag, waiting for the fishing boat to rise enough so I could jump.

I made it, just landing in a heap at the feet of some poor soul. He quickly picked me up and took me down some rusty white stairs to what I could only describe as a filth laden room. Beer cans, old sheets from newspapers, sweet wrappers, even whisky bottles rolling along the floor as the ship pitched up and then back. The smell was like nothing else, sweat, cigarette smoke, and vegetable soup.

Just the thought turned my stomach all over again. Some smells just stay with you throughout life. The smell of the cigarettes just took me straight back to my bed when I was eight. I wonder what my father would think of me now, stuck out in the middle of the North Sea, on a pirate radio ship!

Happy

For the first time in my adult life I was happy. My love for music was a great fit to working on board. I didn't have my own radio time slot at first.

I would sit in for the others when they were too hung over, or on shore leave; or what often happened, they just did not wake up in time, I would be there.

The ship itself was extremely haunted. You can imagine how much fun there was to be had with practical jokes, wind ups and of course the odd unexplained ghostly happening.

The jokes were all a part of relieving the boredom. Ten men and one woman cook, living together with very little to do.

Newspapers would often self-combust, flames would jump up and set the water sprinklers off. It would be a weekly event. Clingfilm on the toilet was another favourite. I learnt fast to always check.

Years later a film was made about radio Caroline called 'The Boat that Rocked', we all knew it as 'the boat that stunk'!

Most of the paranormal activity consisted of stories like the one of the missing crew member. The story went that a man in his early twenties had fallen over board during a rather fierce gale and his body never found, however you could hear his footsteps up on deck during calm weather. I never knew if this was true but I can remember one of the Canadian disc jockeys being spooked out when he claimed the face of a man peered at him through his port hole window (the window was on the outside of the ship with no access from outside). The poor man was really rather shook up, and he believed he had seen a ghost.

Then there was the record library. This was a large room at the bow, wall to wall with vinyl. Just about any record you would ever want was in that library.

One morning I heard music coming from that room, yet no one was anywhere near. It was like the records were playing themselves! I can still remember the track, David Bowie Jean Jeanie. Even for me there are things which I cannot find an explanation for.

I shared a cabin for the first three months with an American DJ called Dave Black. He was not that sociable, he smoked and drank, but never took drugs. One rule on board, if you were caught with drugs that was you out.

The beds were hammocks, stretched out over a metal frame. I was normally so tired by the time I went to bed I never really noticed the discomfort until I woke the following day with a stiff back and shoulder. I was in the top bunk, wedged into a small space, just big enough to crawl under two rather grubby blankets. The cabin was so cold. There was a small port hole just below me. That was why Dave took the lower bunk, he could see out across the water, which was just water, but he was senior and also alpha. I was not going to argue with Mr. Black. (Later we became close friends staying in touch for many years.)

Dave was not much of a talker for a radio DJ. He would nod, or point, gesture or just grunt. Few words seldom left his lips. Until one early morning.

I woke to Dave's foot kicking my backside, "wake up" "wake up" he shouted in a hushed tone, hardly baring to open his mouth. The cabin was lit up by two very bright balls of light, the size of a small rubber bouncy ball. The orbs floated for a while in the middle of the room before making an exit through the metal hull of the ship and out over the sea. We both sat and watched them dumb founded through the tiny port hole window. The lights reflecting on the calm sea, shimmering on the water as they disappeared over the dark horizon.

You know when a person who doesn't believe has an experience which they cannot find a logical explanation for? This was Dave.

I believe we both witnessed 'orbs' that morning. An orb is an intelligent life form that travels vast distances in search for other intelligent life. Now I might argue that no life in our cabin was intelligent! But these small concentrated balls of light may well have been as surprised to encounter us, as we were them. Why would anyone be living in the middle of the North Sea?

My six months went by in a flash, at no time did I regret choosing to go on board. I still have friends today thirty five years later that still work in radio; a brilliant experience which prepared me for the next chapter of my life. I was joining up. But first I had a couple of old friends to catch up with.

Endings

I know in life nothing lasts forever, and that things come in groups of three. My time at the radio station had now come to a close. Six months had gone by in a heartbeat and I was gathering up my belongings ready to make the four hour sea journey back to the east coast. I had no place which I could call home. Hotel and B & B rooms would have to do for a few days.

My first duty was to visit Cathy. I had promised I would call in on my way to R.A.F. training in Lincolnshire. It would be one last chance to see all my friends at the church.

I called John from my hotel. These were the days of call boxes, no mobile phones (not that private and you had to have a stack of ten pence pieces so when the pips went you could buy more conversation time.)

I can recall having a long chat with John. My tall stack of money was all gone when I replaced the black 'Bakelite' hand set on the grey pay phone.

I told him that I had a few days before I had to go again, arranging to meet the following Saturday so I could watch the evening service with him.

I wanted to surprise Cathy. I knew I could not stay with her, my room was now rented out to a student. A young girl who had snapped it up.

Walking down Elizabeth Avenue was strange, the road felt different, or was it just that I had come a long way in eighteen months? I walked up to the front door, same brass door knocker I had used all those months ago, but this time nothing, I knocked again thinking Cathy must have fallen asleep. But again nothing. Could she have gone out? I asked myself. 'Cathy never goes out' I thought.

Feeling a little confused, I thought I would try her neighbours. 'The Gordons' - lovely people, he had been a bank manager, now retired, his wife a professional dance teacher.

The moment Mr. Gordon saw me standing at the door, his face dropped, I was not expecting that. My thoughts raced.
"You better come in." He said, "Cup of tea?" I nodded. Now I knew something was wrong.

Bone china cup and saucer, filled with steaming hot Earl Grey tea, a treat!

Mr. Gordon continued, "You here to see Cathy?" I nodded, almost in expectation of being told she had moved or just popped out for the day, but I knew before the words came out of his mouth. "I'm sorry but Cathy died two weeks ago." "We did not know where you were, so we could not tell you." "Her funeral was yesterday, you missed it by a day."

This news took a moment to sink in, she had not come through to me, but then why would she? Sometimes you just have to accept that you're not that important.

I drank my tea, said my goodbyes and left, the last time I ever walked along that avenue. I felt more tearful about Cathy than I ever had about my father. But then again she had been a friend when I had need of someone, friendship never dies.

I had one last person to call in on before I left my home city and started a new life.

John had been my friend, like Cathy. He was there for me during times of trouble. I always looked forward to spending time with him. Our conversations would be about everything from reincarnation all the way to Alien planets and the universe.

I had always been interested in these subjects. As a young boy I would go into second hand book shops and buy UFO books. I was under the age of ten. My father was very much closed, so John was the first adult who I discussed my passions with. I loved our debates.

The notice board was still on the wall next to the blue door, the narrow entrance, leading to the massive church.

This was my home, everybody knew me, but on this day as I walked in out of the bright spring sunshine the place felt empty.

Every Tuesday John would be downstairs 'healing'. He would have a line of familiar faces sitting patiently waiting. But no line, no John!

Mary who was always somewhere to be found cleaning, or arranging the flowers was in the tiny kitchen. I can remember her giving me the warmest of hugs, the sort of hug that you get when someone is upset.

"John not in yet?" I asked, innocently.

Mary looked at me, then smiled, "haven't you heard? John died three weeks ago".

I froze, my whole body stopped, everything went still for a split second. Then I heard myself saying, - "John could not have died, I only spoke with him on the phone two days ago."

"You must be mistaken", "John passed over three weeks last Friday", Mary continued, "a stroke, followed by a heart attack". Everyone is very upset, no one can get him through. It's just like he went without saying goodbye."

"But Mary" I stuttered, "I only spoke with him on the phone two days ago, we had a long conversation about how life moves on at times when you least expect it." "We had arranged to meet today, that is why I am here, Saturday service, and to have dinner with John."

Hard to believe the events of that day. I knew I had spoken with John, he was his normal cheerful self, full of positive thoughts, and very excited for me that my life was going in a good direction. John was a force of nature. One of a kind and the kindest man I ever knew. If anyone could manage to arrange a phone call from spirit, it would be him. And that is what I believe he did. I know what took place, the conversation, the money spent, the pips, the time and date to meet up, all happened. I just wished I had known he was in spirit! So many questions.

I look back at my time with both Cathy and John and wonder whether or not they were Earth Angels. People sent to this realm to help those in need. I certainly needed help when they both came into my life. I honestly believe I would not be here now if it was not for them. Life had not seemed worth it after my dad passed. With my beliefs and knowledge I could have easily moved myself over. It had occurred to me, then I met Cathy, and shortly afterwards John. I am no one special, we all go through hard times in our lives, but I have learnt that it is the people you meet who make the difference, Cathy and John, two very special souls.

Time Slips

Have you ever thought what life would be without time? If you were to look in a dictionary time would be explained as 'a measurement for the purpose of order'. In fact time is such an integral part of our lives we would be lost without the 24 hour clock. From the very beginning man has been looking for ways to place order into life. From the sundial to the hourglass - all the way to modern crystal quarts driven time pieces dividing up the moments for our own convenience. But is 'time' a precise science? How could it be? It is only the way we order our lives. Time is a manmade concept that we want to accept as a constant. But what if it is not? What if we could dip in and out of 'time' at will? Or just by chance? What if time did not exist in the way we think it does? We just believe time the way it is because it is all we have ever known.

Making sense of all the theories could take a life time! I would like to draw your attention to some events that challenge the concept of time. Events that would be very hard to explain if you think of time as a straight line. (For example one event leads to another that leads to another). We would be on a fixed journey from birth, starting from the moment we were born, ending the day we pass on to spirit.

This is how my concept of time was until I started discovering people who had experiences with places or events which could not be explained by time being a constant. These experiences pointed to time being a 'circle' not a straight line. If time was a circle we could dip in and out of the present. Maybe at will or by pure chance, just by being in the right place at the right 'time'. The very fact that time has no 'beginning nor end' is hard enough. But when time does not act in the way we expect it opens up a different way of seeing time.

The following stories are true, told to me by ordinary people who were just living their lives when something happened to them to make them ask the question. Could it be possible to slip either forward or back in time?

This first event happened in the late seventies. John was an ordinary man. His life revolved around working and looking after his elderly mother. Every Saturday he would turn on his small black and white television, settle back and watch the afternoon sport. This was his time, which no one would interfere with. At one o'clock he turned on his television to find the normal programming changed to make room for a breaking news story.

The power station which he passed every day on his way to work had exploded. Several people had been badly injured. The pictures showed black smoke pouring from the building. Fire Engines, ambulances and police cars surrounding the scene. It was like watching a disaster movie.

The news programme finished and the normal Saturday afternoon sports took over. John thought nothing more about this until six o'clock.

Deciding to put the news back on for an update, he was surprised to see nothing more was said about the power station. Thinking this was rather strange he phoned his bother. The conversation was rather odd. John asked his brother if he had seen the earlier news about the explosion. And although his brother had watched the same one o 'clock news he had seen nothing out of the ordinary. John was left confused, he had no way of working out what had happened. Had he dreamt the whole thing? It wasn't until the following Saturday that the very same news flash was on again. This time John phoned his brother straight away. His brother was watching in disbelief. Had John foreseen the events from the power station one whole week before they happened? If there is another explanation I would really like to hear it.

Story two is a little less dramatic but nevertheless just a baffling. Neil Adams, the current Manager of football championship side Norwich City had an experience that he can offer no explanation for. As a young professional footballer Neil was always nervous the night before a game. Sleeping could be difficult. But as Neil recalls this night he had no trouble getting to sleep. In a very clear cognitive dream Neil was in the middle of the game he was about to play the following afternoon. He could see the bright blue sky, the white cotton wool clouds, even the faces of the spectators behind the goal. In his dream he was standing behind the ball about to take a free kick on the edge of the opponent's penalty box. He could see the sky, the faces of the opposite team which stood before him, even the green of the goalkeeper's jersey. He placed the white ball down very carefully before curling it up and over the wall beyond the stretching grasp of the goalkeeper into the top left-hand corner of the goal. Neil felt the rush of adrenaline as the leather ball smacked against the back of the net. The crowd roared then Neil woke up. It had all been a dream. The next day was match day. Neil can't remember too much about the game until the second half when his team won a free kick on the edge of their opponent's penalty box. In a flash the moment came back to him, the same sky, the same faces, everything was like it had been the night before. He carefully placed the ball down, like he had done in his dream, looked at the same green jersey on the goalkeeper, Neil just knew the outcome even before he had kicked the ball, Neil 'knew' he was about to score, the order of events happened just as he had visualised the night before in his dream, only this time he scored for real, a surreal moment that Neil has never forgotten.

So did Neil go forward in time to watch an event happen 12 hours in advance, before he made it happen? Again I'm willing to listen to any alternative explanations. I personally believe that dreams can lead us to making the correct choices, especially if you consider that everything which has happened is already in the consciousness. If the universe stores events, then what's stopping us accessing 'The Future'? Dreams are sometimes the only way to gain this knowledge. Our daily lives do not always allow us to think about the future. When we sleep most of us do not have control over where our dreams take us. But some dreams do stand out, remaining clear even after waking, or something triggers the recall. Maybe when we sleep we suspend our human understanding of time. Logic never seems to play a part in the dreams, in fact all the understandings of the things we are told or believe in the waking world can be challenged. Just ask Neil.

The first two examples of time slips were about going forward in time. This next story is about going back in time. In the Charlie Chaplin film 'The Circus.', there is a scene at the beginning where people are filmed walking along a path outside the circus. As the crowd moves along, the camera picks up a person dressed as a woman, her clothes are dark, a long skirt, jacket, hat and very large shoes. Which look odd on a lady. But much more eye catching is what looks like a mobile phone placed to her right ear. This film was made in 1927! Sixty years before mobile technology was available! If you would like to see this for yourself you can by going to 'YouTube', put in 'Charlie Chaplin time traveler'. Watch it for yourself, I have many times, but still can't think of a logical explanation. One post script to this story. I have tried to buy a copy of this film on D.V.D. and whilst all of Charlie Chaplin's films are still available 'The Circus' is not. Just wonder why this would be?
So by now you might be questioning what time is. How relevant time is to us? Could we change the course of our lives if we really do get a glimpse of the future?

The simple answer is yes. To understand the future is to make the right choices now. In this next example something as simple as a piece of music can warn us about an event that is about to happen.

Why do you think you like one thing better than another? For example, music can be full of personal memories. But what if those memories were not just from this life time? If you consider that you may live many life times, some things common to you today in your current life will still be familiar to you from past lives and even future lives. The sun has always been there. Bird song, the sea, landscapes, things throughout history which have never changed. We may go from life to life but nature stays the same.

The 'Ground Hog' theory suggests that we can be placed in a time loop. This means we would live the same life time, many times over. Events could become very familiar. (Deja vous, or the feeling of knowing something you shouldn't.) That inner voice saying "no, don't do that." We have all experienced this. But could it be because we have already suffered from the consequence of making a wrong choice? Or choosing to be in the wrong place at the wrong time cutting our life short?

Let me introduce you to Mike.

Mike is a very ordinary man, he has a wife and 3 children, married for the last 20 years and lives in a 3 bedroom semidetached house just outside London, England.

Mike is not spiritual, he has only a little knowledge of religion, mainly through school. His main concerns are looking after his family.

Mike's job is pretty laborious, he drives for a living. Up and down the motorways of Great Britain trying to sell insulation products to various building companies.

A man that you just would not notice, living a life which thousands of others live.

I would not normally meet Mike, our lives are miles apart, but something happened to him on one very ordinary day, something which he just could not understand, or explain.

This is Mike's story in his own words:

'I got up for work like usual at 6am. I had a long way to drive as I was heading up the A1 motorway from my home on the outskirts of London to Yorkshire. This was a journey that I would do at least once a month. I knew the roads with a monotonous regularity, endless double carriage ways packed with lorries and trucks, bending and twisting as the road wielded its way from south to north.

The journey would take 3 hours (as long as there were no hold ups.)

Driving was dull and boring. I could feel myself drifting off from time to time, so to remedy this I had installed in my brand new black Vauxhall estate a radio which had a connection for an 'M.P.3 player'. This tiny little piece of technology was a life saver, who could imagine I could download all of my music onto such a device? Well over 700 tracks from all my favourite pop music albums!

I would plug in my M.P.3 at the beginning of my journey, press 'random' and just let it play in any order. I never got bored because I would always try to guess what the next track would be. Of course I had my own individual album tracks which I loved. Funny how those tracks would come up less often! Random is just that, random, a one in 700 chance of hitting any individual song.

My very favourite track and one that meant a lot to me was Led Zeppelin's 'All of my Love'. The extended studio version. This track never did seem to come up. I would wait weeks just to hear it, often slowing down or stopping to enjoy the whole song in its entirety. Over the months Led Zeppelin had become a special event when selected by my tiny silver musical box.

Picture the scene, bright sunny spring morning, the sun behind me as I drove up the ever busy A1 to my destination. I was making good time, M.P.3 player plugged in and doing its job. I was about an hour away from my first appointment, which I knew I would be on time for.

Then the familiar sound of 'Robert Plant', 'Jimmy Page', and 'John Paul Jones' started playing. My heart jumped and the widest smile came over my face, 'today was going to be a good day', I thought to myself as I prepared to make the most of the music. For once I did not slow down, I was aware of my deadline and wanted to be on time.

The track ran for 7 minutes 59 seconds in which time I had travelled another nine or ten miles.

Then something happened that had never previously happened before, my random M.P.3 player choose at random the same track! Led Zeppelin - 'All of my Love!' Once was incredible, but to repeat the same track again, at random was unheard of.

I slowed right down from 70 mph, to 45 mph, and pulled over into the slow lane, I could hardly believe my own ears!

And then without warning a lorry carrying a load of steel girders shed its load right in the place where my car had been moments earlier. If I had been driving at my normal speed, in the middle lane I would have been right behind that lorry. I no doubt would have been crushed underneath 3 twelve foot steel beams that now lay in the middle lane of the A1!

Everything happened in slow motion, one minute I was singing along, the next moment I could not believe my ears, then the lorry depositing the steel girders.

I have thought about this moment many times since. Could it just have been three random acts occurring together? Just coincidence? My favourite track which had not come up in months, coming up not just once, but twice. The lorry at that precise moment losing its load. Then the fact I had slowed down moments before. I would never have normally done that. It took my M.P 3 player to do something which it had never done before to get my attention.

Could the combination of my M.P.3 player, Led Zeppelin and my reaction to the double play of my favourite song have saved my life? All of these events were random, all had to come together in the right order, only then would the outcome be good.'

I have heard different stories like Mike's, where random events have saved a life. Could it be that we live the same life time over and over again? If something stops us, if we make the wrong choices, we just go right around again until we realise? Could our lives be on a 'time loop' which keeps repeating until we have fulfilled our destiny, or current life purpose? Maybe this is why we get that feeling of having done something before? Or that knowing deep inside that what we are doing is not going to work out well?

We could have made the same mistakes infinitely.

The signs are there if we wish to stop and take notice, even if we do not realise why we are stopping.

Future Foretold

Just before I joined the RAF, I went to see a palmist.

I believed in many things, most of them things I had experienced whilst actively engaged in finding out about anything paranormal. I took a really keen interested in ghosts, time travel and strange areas on this planet, like the Bermuda Triangle.

I have to admit I am slightly sceptical of predictions of the future.

35

At my young age I could not see how time could be anything other than a straight line from the day you were born until the day you went on that short journey across the thin divide.

Fate had no real meaning, I believed you made your own destiny by the choices you made. Self-responsibility. Well I was only just twenty one with my own strong opinions.

Here I am, sat in this rather strange room, curtains drawn, spotlight focused on my right hand, which in turn was rested on a small green felt table.

The man sat directly across the table from me and was old! Simply old. Metal rimmed glasses, hair swept back across his much furrowed brow.

This encounter was going to be one of the strangest, and looking back some of the most accurate predictions I was going to be witness to. In fact, if I had not taped this I would not have believed one man could get so much right. Not that I knew that at the time, hindsight is a wonderful thing.

Now I am not a fortune teller. But I can read people. Faces will give most people away.

I saw this man noticeably react to seeing my palm. A mixture of shock, amazement and wonder; mixed up in a split second. I caught his eyes as he glanced upwards.

It was then that I realised my hand was unique.

"You understand that palmistry is not an exact science don't you?" I nodded. I did not understand what lines and contours could show. This stuff was made up from knowledge previously learnt from books and readings.

He continued, "You my boy have a very rare hand." "You have three life lines, something that I have never seen before." He now had my attention. "Each line depicts separate lives." "Your first life, has already ended before your teenage years had finished." (He was right, my father had died when I was nineteen and my life had changed beyond all recognition, because of circumstances out of my control.)

"Your second life will last two decades, before another dramatic change happens". (I did not know or have any idea what he was predicting.) But how right he was, to the year!

After I joined up I spent twenty years away from spiritualism. My life was ruled by duty and family commitments. The person I was 'submerged in officialdom'. Lost in a maze of pleasing others and financial gain.

36

He continued gathering pace and vigour in his voice, "you will not find true happiness until your early forties."

Again he was right.

I was still in my early forties when I left the military world behind, devoiced my then wife, left my home and moved into my two bedroom flat. At the same time I started working for myself, as a professional psychic. I had never been so happy. Each day was an adventure. Yes I might be broke, but boy was I happy. It was as he had predicted on the tape all those years ago, my third life time was about to start.

And my first job as a professional psychic medium, was Ghost - House.

Two words that I have come to dread

'Only Joking'
Sitting in a coffee house, man bangs into my chair, then says, 'you should have moved' Now being the calm gentle man that I am now I stood up!
The man then said - 'Only Joking!'
I had a mind to put his walking stick somewhere where he would never lose it.
But instead I said 'Hello Joe nice to meet you!'
Words, clichés can be most frustrating. I have tried to cut out using 'you know' and the fabulous 'what do you mean?' Language is diverse, it is wonderful, spoken in accents which denote regions. So why use cliché phrases and words? Talk properly please, and never ever say 'only joking' when you have meant every word you have just said.

CORNER CAFÉ

September 2016 was a very busy and exciting month for Dominic and myself. We were in Australia hosting seminars and teaching in Brisbane, Queensland, enjoying the lovely hot spring.

We arrived, jet lagged on a Saturday, delighted we had Sunday to recover before starting on the following Monday.

Brisbane is situated in a region I can only describe as 'basin shaped', downhill with all the businesses and shops together, surrounded by a picturesque river and moorings.

There was lots to explore, so we set off downhill to the city centre. I had always expected Brisbane to be bustling and full of people from all over the world, walking 'fast paced' on mobile phones. Well on this particular day the opposite was true. Yes, it was Sunday and Australia's 'Father's Day' but it was so quiet and tranquil. Hardly a cloud in the sky, only the odd squawk of birds in the trees which edged the park. In fact it almost seemed ghost like, surreal and not at all how I'd imagined the city to be.

We continued our walk past beautifully landscaped botanical gardens until we reached Kind Edward Street. We noticed many of the streets were named after our Kings and Queens, with lots of brass signposts giving clear directions.

We ambled along, almost alone on these fairly empty streets, looking for a coffee shop. Large stores were still to open, so we continued along King Edward Street which connected to a few others leading to a junction. I remember seeing a flock of pure white cockatoos flying freely overhead and wishing I had remembered my camera.

We then noticed a tall, upright church on the corner, with a sharp spire on top, making a note of this as our 'Landmark' for when we walked back to the hotel.

Luckily we had stopped right next to a very small corner café. Hardly room for eight people, with a couple of tables and chairs outside.

Had we not stopped to look at the cockatoos we would probably have walked by and missed it altogether. We were both shattered so went inside and sat down by the small window. There was a girl we spotted behind the counter whose accent was Liverpudlian! I remember looking at the cakes displayed, not really taken by any of them, but needed something to nibble on. The girl chatted to us and said this was a 'family business' and everything homemade. She was very chatty and told us her grandfather had emigrated when he was younger, and had been a miner, then had an accident and needed his leg amputated, then opened up the café.

The girl somehow seemed out of place behind the counter serving and I felt she was a people person who really wanted to be elsewhere. She was very interest to hear we were from England and wanted to know why we were here and for how long. Anyway we ordered two coffees, one black in the tiniest of cups you could imagine. A white for me and a piece of hard baked tiffin cake which nearly broke my teeth and tasted stale. Not one to complain (especially as the girl was so friendly) I had one bite, got a napkin and covered the rest as a child might do. The atmosphere at the café was strange, we were the only people inside, but a couple sat outside adjacent to the church with the spire. It was unlike any place I had been to before. An unkempt, rather old man came in as we were leaving and slumped into the corner. I noticed the young girl knew him and brought him a piece of the 'Tiffin Cake'. Good luck with that I thought!

We paid the extremely cheap bill and told the girl we would probably call in later during the week.

Tired, we decided to go back to the hotel (uphill now!) which was a good forty minutes' walk.

We had a much needed sleep that night followed by a few very busy days working around the hotel, only allowing a few hours of sunbathing on our balcony.

The schedule on Wednesday was shorter than previous days so we had some free time later in the day to explore Brisbane a little more.

We again walked down the long hill, however the atmosphere was very different. It was busy and bustling, the city come to life, unlike the previous Sunday. As you can imagine there are many sky rise buildings within Brisbane, a young city, very cosmopolitan!

We did the 'tourist route', with a boat ride across the river, and the 'city tour bus', allowing lots of relaxation.

We decided to find the street off King Edward Street again, and call into the café before we went back. It was Wednesday afternoon ('Hump day' as it's called in Australia!) hot, busy, with buses and taxis everywhere. We hadn't taken note of the café's name but knew it was adjacent to the church with the spire, which had been our 'landmark'.

Everything this day seemed different, people on phones walking fast, cyclists weaving in and out of traffic, lots of people pushing push chairs in our direction.

We spotted our 'landmark' in the distance standing majestically high in the city skyline. I wondered to myself if the Liverpudlian girl would still be there, wanting a long conversation again.

As we crossed at the traffic lights on approach to the café we could see children on the corner, waving balloons, blocking the footpath. A brightly coloured clown stood there, blowing up balloons in various shapes and animals, to the sheer delight of the children. No wonder lots of pushchairs were going in that direction. Dominic and I had to stop to allow them to pass by.

The clown finished, picked up his rucksack and walked ahead of us, into the café, as we followed.

Suddenly, as we entered, we stopped in our tracks – we weren't in a café, but a Joke shop! Extremely baffled we came out and looked around. The church was there as before, but no tables or chairs were outside, just a few 'popped' balloons and mothers talking on the corner.

We decided to go back in the shop and ask where the café was, or had it changed hands in just a few days? The diameter of the shop was exactly the same as before, except rows of fake moustaches and 'squirty' water pistols had replaced the hard baked cakes. There was no girl, just an elderly man behind the counter. I asked about the corner café, but he didn't recall a café ever being there! He said the joke shop had been there for many years!

We were completely confused; we knew we sat down here a few days before, by the small window looking out onto the church; and had seen no joke shop. How can a café disappear? We knew we were in the correct place.

Mentally drained and tired, we got a taxi back to our hotel, making neither head nor tail of what had happened.

The following Sunday we retraced our steps again to see if we would find the café. But no luck, we couldn't. No one seemed to know of its whereabouts.

We were a month in Brisbane and we never came across it again, making us question 'where was it'? 'What had we experienced'?

Just maybe we had gone into another era, or 'time warp'. Who knows?

This was certainly for us 'No joke'!

Alison Zenden

Meeting

I have heard it said we will meet up to 80,000 people during our life. Only a very few of these people will ever become special. I will sit and think about all the people in the world. Look at all the television aerials going past whilst on the train, and think that each house has a story, a family. Hard to relate to all the people.
From a country of 45,000, back in the fifteenth century, to a country which has around 70 million today! Where have all the souls come from?
The answer is simple. Like most things in the universe. Billions of planets, trillions of souls, spread out across the cosmos. Each planet evolving then dying in turn. An ever changing kaleidoscopic landscape of life.
Just consider the possibility that your soul could have lived on many separate occasions, on many different planets. Millions of life times. Just this life is on this tiny blue dot in the corner of our Galaxy. Not so hard to understand 'the soul' and its journey when you look up, or down, or to the side. Home planets are abundant.

CHAPTER THREE

New Day

Each and every day when I awake I never know what may occur.

Today was one of those days. It started off very routine, a trip to the shops. Had a few things on my mind to buy, now shopping for me is very dull, supermarkets scare me. I always have to search for the things l need. But there is always a good side to everything if you care to look for it. For me it's second hand shops. I loved looking round old furniture, books long forgotten, old items which would have looked good in homes of the fifties and sixties. I really could spend hours just picking up items using psychometry to transport myself back in time. My youngest son will sometimes join me routing through old records, boxes of junk.

I remember looking at a rather smart jacket, weighing up whether to buy it or not.

Holding the garment up to my son asking "What do you think"? "That's nice dad, but do you think somebody died in it"! Well that was it l just fell about laughing. I now can't go into a second hand shop without thinking 'somebody might have passed over' wearing or using the items laid out in front of me! My son has much to learn about spirit, but l always hope he keeps his sense of fun.

That's why l love life. You just never know what might be round the corner. Today was going to be one of those days. One of my last jobs before returning home was to visit the florists. I always like to have fresh flowers in my home, just waking up to the natural scent would fill my heart with joy. My usual shop was shut, so l decided to call in on the next nearest, so pleased l did. You know that feeling when the hairs stand up on the back of your neck? That's how l felt as l walked in through the rather stiff front door. A little bell tinkled as the door swung shut, almost like somebody had grabbed it out of my hand. A friendly lady stood in front of me, big smile on her face "don't worry" she smiled, "that happens all the time", she went on, "it's only our resident ghost Charlie"! "He just likes to be noticed, if he didn't like you he wouldn't let you in". In my head l' m thinking now l know why l came, just knew l had to explore. Charlie was now in my head.

My glance wondered around the small rather untidy shop, the floor was scattered with buckets full of every type of floral adornment you could imagine. The smell was overwhelming, above all the scent of Lillie's, my favourite, I love watching them unfold then the scent lasts forever, always guaranteed to fill my tiny flat, making me feel I'm at home. I choose a big bunch shaking the water from the bottom of the stems and handing them over.

With ease the lady wrapped them in light pink and white paper, I just couldn't help myself, I had to ask her about Charlie, it didn't matter how long it took, I just wanted to know, hoping that I hadn't overstepped the mark.

I need not have worried. This was one lady who was happy to share her experiences. Charlie has always been a part of this place, she started, "I have owned this little shop for over forty years, it was always busy with people coming and going, I have seen generations of families get married, and buried, when I think back I must have sold fresh flowers to Charles family for more years than I care to think back. Charlie was the first owner of the shop at the turn of the century, the shop was a green grocers, and I mean a green grocer. Fresh vegetables grown locally; very little fruit, mainly apples and pears. Oranges weren't heard of, unlike today people lived a very simple existence never wanting for much.

The local families knew each other. Most had been born at home and played in the streets surrounding the little line of shops. Grew up, worked together in the local community, there was very little outside influence. So hard to imagine in these days of jet travel and motor cars." So inside 'Florrie's shop' was like a time capsule with all the original features, down to the brass bell hung above the door on a piece of blackened string. Unchanging since the start of time. Charlie wasn't moving, he was right in the centre of my mind, and I just knew he felt the shop was still his. Some spirits never want to move. I often feel it must be like Groundhog Day for them, going over the same routine day after day not wanting to know, nor realising what it means to be in spirit. As a medium this is something you have to come to terms with. It's not alright to rescue all and sundry regardless of whether others wished it. What right do I have to move a spirit on? It's a very personal way of thinking; life is not that complicated it's only people who make it that way. So like Charlie, when we come to the end of one life time why should we do what others want? We surely wouldn't during our lives. Now Charlie was very good at showing he was around. I know that day I was almost pulled through the shop door.

I have no doubt Charlie wanted to show he was still around. He would also play little jokes on the people in the flower shop. For instance at the beginning of the day there would be ten pairs of scissors on the counter near the till, a flower shop without scissors would be like a tea shop with no cakes. Anyhow by the end of the day all the scissors would be gone, nowhere to be seen! Not possible well not in the "normal" world but this used to happen at least every other week, but this isn't the surprising part. The next morning the lady would come down from the small flat above the shop and find all the scissors together on the shop counter by the till just left in a pile! This was Charles' way of saying take notice of me I'm here. This little shop was so interesting, full of activity and it had one more surprise for me, something in all my years of working as a medium had never come across.

Voices in the Air

I have been used to listening to voices in my head, sometimes I just wish I could have a day when spirit doesn't come through. Over the years I have learnt to hold several conversations at the same time, this is a very handy skill when you're on television with another voice in your ear from the producer, but in everyday life it becomes a pain. So you can imagine my surprise when standing in the little shop I heard a male voice about a foot away seemingly coming from thin air. It stopped me in my tracks I just was not used to this type of spirit communication. I needed to listen more and what I could hear was a man's voice talking in a strange tongue, the sound was coming from the telephone line attached to the wall just above my left ear about a foot away! I have studied electronic voice phenomenon (EVP) but had never heard a voice being made audible by a piece of telephone wire. In this day of modern technology we are never far away from being able to record or tape the happenings occurring near us, so I managed to catch a few seconds on my mobile phone, not only to share with others but also for myself, just so I knew I had experienced the voice, and not dreamt it! I took the recording to a friend who had studied history and he recognised the language as old English about 1600's, I thought it was a foreign language, it sounded so different to modern day English.

To me this is just another way spirit keep me interested in understanding the way they can communicate across the centuries with us. I'm always being told 'no such thing as time', it's just a human way of complicating things. For me it was a wakeup call. I was so used to hearing voices in my head it took something like this to help me understand that spirit will use any means possible to get us to recognise that being in 'spirit form' isn't that different from living on Earth as a mortal, with all the challenges it involves. Spirit are only an arm's length away from where we are, and it took a visit to this little shop to remind me, which gets me to the next stage of my life, understanding knowledge of how people are.

Stage

One of the most rewarding (but mind-numbingly nervous) things that I do is work on stage. I have always been a very private person, so you can imagine how much courage it takes just to walk out in front of people, all waiting, wondering, hoping, almost willing for a message. I have never thought of myself as anything special so all those people looking directly at me can be a little thought provoking. "What if nothing comes through?" is always my first thought, which for me as a positive thinker is unthinkable! Then I start the first link, always helps me lift the energy in the theatre; people will laugh whilst listening with intent, hanging on every word, which in turn reminds me of the responsibility of doing this work. I feel very proud that people on both sides of life trust me with the messages which show so much from spirit, as well as sharing the main message which is "life after life." Although I have always had the knowledge that life is eternal ever since I first saw my best friend Katie knocked over by a lorry when very young, then had my Grandfather George come to me all in a very short space of time. I believe because I have experienced these and many more things over the course of my life I don't expect others to see the spirit world as I do, in fact I expect others to question, just like I would if I were sat in their place. Why should we just have faith? It makes no sense, I have always wanted to explore, but I'm never prepared to just believe because somebody tells me to. That's why when I'm on stage it's for me to work as hard as possible to connect the two sides of life together, giving the details without asking any questions. I also believe that everyone in the theatre has a message waiting. It's the skill of the medium to deliver the right message to the right people, and get around as many people as possible. During my shows I will make 25 or more links in the two hours on stage. I give the message then move on to the next person.

I get very upset when I see mediums asking questions, repeating themselves and changing information around. I will give you an example. Watching a medium working with a lady in the audience the conversation went this way. Medium - "Spirit, are telling me you have a tattoo, is this right?" Lady - "No, I haven't." Medium - "Well, I 'm being told you should get one." I don't know how that sounds to you but to me it's such a good example of bad mediumship. It's no wonder people find it difficult to believe. When mediums work they should be direct, honest, and only give what they get from the spirit person.

I would like to think all people are good. In my work as a psychic medium and in more recent years as a healer I have come across some of the kindest folk you would ever wish to meet. People who give their time unconditionally in the service of others. Unsung hero's helping, not because they seek rewards, but simply because they want the world to be a better place. I like to step out of the mortal body which consumes all of our thinking and take a good look around, it's amazing what you see. The world is a wonderful place full of miracles which we miss because we are too wrapped up in our day to day life. I'm no exception to this.

Frogs

My daily routine can make me tired. Some days an endless trail of people wanting private sittings. I never mind because that's why I work as a medium, not to prove anything but to highlight the evidence so people can make up their own minds. Every sitting is different. Take the young man who walked up the stairs to my flat with a wide white smile on his face. Lovely man but I could see sorrow in his deep blue eyes. As usual first thing I do is put the kettle on. "Tea or coffee?" I shout from my small kitchen. "Tea please, very strong." Well, I know as soon as the young man sits down he has a hundred questions all in his mind at the same time, plenty of time to answer after, but right now all l wanted to do was bring this spirit lady through. She had followed him up my stairs, I knew that was why this particular person had searched me out. I expect people to be sceptical but this man was so worried about what he might experience he just couldn't sit down and relax. This was one of those times when I knew only the very best evidence would be enough to keep him interested but might also show him there was another side to life which wasn't easy to except if you wanted to keep within common beliefs.

I wasn't about to challenge him in any way but this lady just wouldn't wait, why should she. She had been waiting for a chance to show her boyfriend that she had never left his side. In my head I had this vision of two people laying down on a blanket looking up at the moon, a river running by their toes with little inserts buzzing just above their heads. It was a late summer evening, two people very much in love, tears were rolling down my cheeks as I describe the picture which was surrounding me. I was no longer in the room, I was on that river bank sharing what was a very private moment, with a bump I was back in the room. The man was sitting opposite with tears also rolling down his face. "How did you know that?" he asked with a puzzled looked etched on his face. It was just like sharing a scene from a film with him, only this film was his life and what I had described was a moment he had often thought about over the last two year since his wonderful girlfriend had passed away, but hadn't left him. These moments are why I work publicly. I don't want much from what I am able to do; but to give definite proof of life after life is a very strong motivation.

The sitting lasted another 2 hours. I never put a time limit on sittings. When I feel like stopping I do. The lady in question brought through a lot more information, including proof of where she had lived, her family and one very funny moment when she described a frog! Big eyes with a bright green skin on top of the television, this was the last gift her boyfriend had given her before she went into hospital. This to me is what it means to be a medium, nothing more or less.

Beliefs.

The realm of spirit is a separate dimension to our current home, 'The Earth'. I believe we are just passing through, but this raises a few questions. When I work as a link, or a medium for 'spirit', I use my mortal self to translate the vibrations from the realm of spirit. Without working out how I do this, I have come to understand that every single atom in the universe vibrates at an individual frequency. My energy field or aura acts as a radio receiver. Whether I like it or not my mortal body is tuned into 'The Realm of Spirit'. I hear voices and sense the energy of the souls who have out lived their mortal bodies and evolve into pure energy consciousness. (We sometimes get to see this pure form of energy in the form of orbs, small round balls of pure white light.)

As a medium, I get no choice, I live with the voices and impressions of spirit twenty-four hours a day. I have no off switch.

We all experience (whether through dreaming, whilst asleep, or in the moments just before losing consciousness) that 'out of body' feeling.

In the following paragraphs I would like to explain in my own words how I have come to understand the purpose of the soul. Please bear in mind this is my truth, I am reluctant to say it is 'the' truth. Many of you will have your own thoughts, theories and beliefs.

Out of Body

Have you ever asked yourself the question "who am I"? I'm sure many of us have questioned who we have become, but this goes deeper even than this. It is the feeling that you are looking in at yourself. This 'out of body' feeling is far more common than we may think. Not easy to explain to anyone who has not experienced this particular sensation, but it could be described as a floating, or light headedness. But what really describes it is being out of synchronisation with your mind or body. For me I have experienced this throughout my life. As a child I would question regularly 'who I was'. The feeling of my body being different from my mind was always within my thoughts. Could it be that the mind and the body are separate? The body just the host? The mind eternal, jumping from body to body with different identities? Nothing in my life up to now would convince me otherwise. This would also explain these 'out of body' shifts of consciousness. Linking the spiritual to the mortal can be confusing but the likelihood is that most of us have had many different bodies with the same consciousness, following us from life time after life time.

This theory opens up many possibilities; it explains why we associate with the familiar. Choosing one direction rather than another. The mind is like a well-trodden path, which is why we recognise those who have shared life times with us. Their body may be different but the sense of knowing that person comes from somewhere deep inside, beyond the psychical. The mind is capable of sensing the vibration each one of us gives out. New theories help us understand the meaning of being 'spiritual'.

We should never stand still. The universe is forever evolving and so should we be. How could we take the knowledge which we already have and grow it unless we challenge that which we have come to believe in, before those who have never thought the same way? I found that growing up in a European country people are slow to face 'new knowledge' preferring to stay with the long known and tested theories. Which is fine by me, if not a little frustrating from time to time. But I have an attitude, a 'never give up' way of thinking which allows me to believe in ground breaking new knowledge which has never been widely accepted. New concepts seem to shed doubt on what has gone before. This to me is evolution, re drawing the dots and challenging how we find our own belief structures. Sharing is as important as breathing. Not because I want you to believe in the same things that I do, but because I would like you to consider that some of the old 'well worn out' concepts are out dated. Re thinking does take effort, but the rewards do come with being at the cutting edge of discovery.

My own understanding comes from inside. It does not come from reading endless books stating the author's point of view written from the point of 'truth'. There is no truth, just each one of us with our own versions. The truth is only relevant to what we believe in. Stop and think about your own beliefs, we rarely change or challenge ourselves. I like to consider carefully who I have become. How did I reach that conclusion? Is my soul so full of understandings when I stop to listen that I do not have to add in what others think to understand? If we do live many life times, and the soul stores every single action, lesson learnt, mistake made, then surely the knowledge which we already have should point us in the right direction.

The Soul

Before we can understand who we may be, we must first learn about 'the soul'. It is very likely that our mortal body is only the outside shell, the disposable part of a nut, the outer casing protecting the precious consciousness of the life energy making us eternal.

Not that much of a leap of faith, the concept of a soul. It makes perfect sense to see every single word action and deed is stored within us. The soul gives a meaning to being alive, to experience. The soul allows us all to learn whilst we live.

Everything is thought. Either starting with a single thought, or triggered by a thought. Long after the body has gone the consciousness of thought is still active.

Could it be that the meaning of life is to experience as many different situations as possible? Navigating around the bad choices to the calmer waters of inner peace; the calm stillness we all feel when all life issues have been resolved?

We know deep down the right and wrong ways to turn, we just ignore the inner voice. The soul is our inner voice, born from thousands, maybe millions of lives where we have learnt lessons the hard way. We are all powerful enough to understand the voice from within.

Think of the soul like a flock of birds. One bird on its own is not that powerful, five or six together have a better chance of making a statement. But millions of birds flying round together is mighty powerful, the whole sky taken over by the ever changing large black shadow as the flock bend and twist their way across the sky.

Our soul is that large flock of birds, each life time representing one single winged object.

The power you have to understand, learn and access the knowledge your soul has gathered is immense and very powerful. You are not just one person making your way through life, you are millions of life time's worth of knowledge stored in the shell of a body with the ability to tap into that stunning consciousness. This is what the soul is designed to do, gather together every single thought, deed and action so you have that knowledge to hand all of the time. Like a mighty flock disguised in a rich orb of energy which we so dismissively call our consciousness.

Let's now try to understand the meaning of having a soul in the context of being eternal.

The pure energy (our soul) is just energy. I could describe the soul in human language, I believe this is a mistake. The realm of spirit is pure thought. This is something many of us in this mortal life struggle to come to terms with.

All we know is what we feel, sense and become aware of whilst living. It stands to reason that we are going to believe the realm of spirit just mirrors the world we currently occupy.

Two main differences between these dimensions.

This mortal world is a world where we act, experience and learn by physically doing. The realm of spirit is a world of memories which we can access by thought.

The two dimensions work together in feeding each existence. In the psychical world everything takes so much consideration. First you have to have the want to do something, then act accordingly, and only then can you achieve your goal. In the realm of spirit thought is all you need to achieve the memory of an action or deed and can be re lived once it has been stored in your soul memory.

Idea

Every single thing you have ever done, or will ever do, will start with a single thought.
Crazy when you stop long enough to think about it.
But where do our thoughts come from? Can thoughts be placed in our minds by spirit?
There are many cases of people waking up from a night's sleep, or dream with inspiration waiting to flow.
When thoughts become action the world becomes different.
For me thoughts are alive. They start cascades of thinking. Their origin? Something to think about.
Either within you, or outside of you, or somewhere we have yet to discover.
Here is the point though; can thought travel? (distant healing) Is the universe crammed full of intelligent life?
What would stop us picking up these thoughts of alien life?
We could all be following orders, believing that everything we think comes from inside.
Now there is something to think about.

CHAPTER FOUR

Ghost House

Looking across the field you could smell the scent of winter. The normally emerald green grass had a white frosting. Autumn was turning into winter. I stood in front of an old bay window. The old wooden frame crumbling, white paint flakes lay on the windowsill, the smell of damp filled my nostrils. This once proud Edwardian house had been neglected for decades, but what a house. I knew it simply as "The Ghost-house." Everything about the house echoed the past, spirits seemed to be encased in the dark wooden floorboards. I could hear the noise of the children playing, running along the narrow corridors; even the smells of food being prepared on the giant Arga in the basement kitchen. This for me as a medium was like being thrown into a large time capsule. I had always considered myself very fortunate, having been able to explore every square inch of this place, unique in England, and maybe even the world.

That morning whilst I had been staring out through the old bay window my thoughts had gone back to the past 4 years. It had been my privilege to be the resident medium for "Ghost-house". I would take groups of eager people round the whole house. From the basement to the loft room. Nothing had been out of bounds. We would sit, huddled together in the cold, damp rooms. Even in summer the rooms would seem cold, waiting for something to happen. We would seldom be disappointed. Today was the last time I would stand in front of this window looking out over the now rather tatty grounds trying to imagine what it might have looked like a hundred and fifty years ago. The owners were selling up. Ghost-house was now a thing of the past. Consigned to history like all the former residents who had once resided in this grand house.

The memories of some remarkable events will stay with me forever. Before I started working at Ghost-house I had been at times sceptical when I had read reports of ghostly sighting. I had always thought it was the person's view of the event that I would hear, embellished to enhance the experience by the teller. I don't want to go too deeply into this, but just remember the last time you told somebody about an event in your life.

You're going to tell the story of that event from your point of view. For example, I have a friend who is a very good healer. She tells the story of helping a man who had burnt his arm (blistering had swollen it.) She told me by placing her hands just above the blisters the arm had become eased and the swelling had gone down. In all a miracle had occurred thanks to her ability to heal. I thought this was very impressive, until I questioned some people who had also been there. They had a different version of what took place. Yes, this lady had held her hands above this poor man's arm, but others had brought ice rapped in tea towels, something this lady had failed to include in her version of events. In other words she had told the story the way she had wanted to remember it. So when people tell me about how they have seen this ghost, or witnessed 'that' event I remember the story of the lady with the healing hands. People only remember what they want to, and will often tell stories in a way that could only ever be deemed as their truth. The only way to experience anything is at first hand. Something I have been very fortunate to do whilst working at Ghost-house.

Looking back I now know why I was placed there. Spirit work in some very strange ways. It was almost like they were saying; "We will teach him to be a sceptic, let's send him to this house in the middle of nowhere". To be honest if I hadn't experienced the things first hand I would not have believed them.

So here are a few of my stories from my own experiences, told in my own words as l remember them...

Lady in the cellar

Most event nights we would get a wide range of people, all from different cultures, backgrounds and professions. My first duty as the 'in house' medium was to take the group of approximately forty people on a tour of the house. I always wanted everyone to feel at home. This tour lasted about an hour, and gave me time to sort the people into four groups of ten. These groups would then be escorted by a member of staff to the first visuals of the night.

Any of you who have been on a haunted tour would know how boring these visuals could be, sitting waiting, watching, taking digital photographs to capture orbs. It was never boring at Ghost-house. I would set up temperature controlled cameras in the rooms. These wonders of technology would then be linked to a computer via a web cam. If the room temperature dropped we would capture any ghostly images on camera. (Room temperature is an indication of paranormal activity; the room can fall as much as 15 c in a matter of seconds when a spirit enters the room.) I had four locations wired up. The Bishops room. The Chinese room. The main Stairway, and back corridor, (a massive oak staircase that was the centre piece of this old Edwardian house.) And the cellar. This room was below the kitchen and the temperature would shift all over the place; but on event nights I would always want to set up a visual in this room because it was by far one of the most haunted locations in the house. The cellar was where my group would go first.

On this one night I introduced myself to my group and asked each member to do the same. My group were all police men and women from the surrounding Derbyshire area. Very nice people as I can remember, mainly sceptical, still open minded.

The temperature camera was set, the web cam ready. I would carry my own temperature gauge, so I could monitor the conditions. A dry summer's night, in the middle of July, the cellar was dark, torches shone, flicking beams of light, catching dusty wooden boxes and beer bottles. As the group settled down and waited for something to happen.

On my right a young man in his twenties, on my left a lady mid-thirties, tall with her blonde hair tied back, no nonsense personality. Without warning the temperature started to drop, the lady next to me started shivering, complaining her feet had gone so cold she could no longer feel her toes. She was right, the temperature in the cellar above her had dropped to an icy minus 5. By now her legs and lower body had frozen, I had to get her out of the cellar and upstairs into the kitchen. With one arm around my shoulder and her other arm around the young man next to her, we carried this poor lady to the top of the stairs. Both her legs were useless. Sitting her down by the kitchen table, next to the warmth of the kitchen stove, her lower body started to warm up and she slowly regained the feeling in her legs, then toes. Excitedly she got back up proclaiming "this is the best thing that has ever happened to me on a ghost hunt, I want to go back down"! It took me all my time to persuade her it might not be a good idea!

By this time the other members of the group had come into the kitchen to find out what was happening. The best way I thought to explain would be to check the footage on the computer. Everything had been recorded. What we all saw next scared the life out of some of the group.

The footage showed us all sitting together, torches flashing. Then this white mist like shadow, drifting first around my feet, then settling on the lap of this lady, just hovering above her jeans, and trainers. It was like watching the mist roll in across the shore on a cold winter's morning. The camera kept rolling as the two of us picked up the lady and dragged her up the stairs.

The room went silent, grown men with blank expressions.

Then laughter, relief that everyone was safe, and everyone talking at once.

The upshot of that night was a visit from 'The Most Haunted' television programme. They filmed at Ghost-house for two days and two nights. The host claimed to have found her guide in one of the rooms. But the house went quiet during filming. Not much was caught on their cameras, still they had my footage of the ghost in the cellar.

Many Rooms

Ghost-house is split up into many rooms, all have a name. One of the most active rooms in the house was "The Bishops" room. I have held many séances in this room with differing results. Some nights the Bishop himself would come through and talk through either myself or a guest medium. We would invite new mediums all the time. This would achieve two things. First it was always good to get a fresh approach to the spirit energy that could be felt. 'The Bishop' would always come through in the same way, no matter which medium brought him into the room. I saw some very kindly lady mediums turn into a red faced angry man; he would take their breath away. I was always very careful not to give anything away to the guest medium. I wanted them to experience the true effect, so l had to stand back and watch, only stepping in if l felt l had to. This happened one night when the medium was so overwhelmed by the spirit of 'The Bishop', a dark spirit who had a sense of occasion. I had to step in and close the séance down. Needless to say that medium never came back. Not because we didn't want her back, but because she couldn't cope with the intense energy of such a spirit. This lady was a very well-known medium who had been working for spirit for many years.

That's how real events revealed themselves once we starting tapping into the forces which were inside the Bishop's room. I would often comment to the owners that the house would become alive again during the all-night events. I'm convinced to this day 'The Bishop' was very much a part of that room and he didn't want to leave. I tried on many different occasions to get this spirit to move on with no success.

The conclusion being that spirit have free will. If they want to be encased in their mortal life, as with "The Bishop", then there is nothing that can be done to move them on. From a personal point of view this makes me feel sad that another senescent life form would choose to stay entrapped in their mortal form, even if it is within a spirit body existence. But I can see why it might happen. I think 'The Bishop' is afraid to move on into the spirit world. His beliefs, his actions, if you like and the way he lived his life prevents him from meeting his very own judgment day. If only he knew the real truth, or should I say *my* real truth I'm sure he would reconsider.

I learned so much from those encounters with the spirit of "The Bishop."

Before I leave the subject of this room, I had one other experience that certainly made me sit up and take notice.

It's very important that we encounter something new, especially when dealing with the paranormal. We look first for all the possible reasons for that situation occurring. So when on one damp rainy afternoon I opened the large oak door to 'The Bishop's' room the last thing I had suspected was to be met by a group of what I can only describe as orbs. Small round balls of light the size of a small rubber bouncy ball. To say I was in total disbelief is an understatement. I must have stood transfixed for what seemed like hours. In fact it must have only been moments, because as I realized what I was witnessing all I wanted to do was count the number of orbs, which in itself was a fruitless exercise. Each orb would move up and down, then side to side. Far too fast to be able to track them individually, making counting them a futile endeavor.

Now up to that time I had only ever seen a couple of orbs (in my cabin on board Radio Caroline) but never a large group like this. Yes I had seen large groups of orbs in photographs, but was convinced they were only moisture trapped in the air, or relaxations of light from windows, or even grains of pollen caught on modern technology. Energy that have always been there, but until recently never seen by the naked eye "if orbs could be explained rationally then they were not paranormal.

I didn't need to look any further." This wasn't one of those times, I could see with my very own eyes lights dancing around. It was a dull afternoon, no sunlight. All l could think was 'wow, these orbs are not dust particles.' Firstly I know orbs are a form of intelligent life. I believe they move by thought, therefore are capable of interaction. I have also come to the conclusion that their purpose is to collect intelligent thoughts. So orbs are connected to the universe's thought process through, "Clair-cognizance" (universal knowledge.) The more l think about this the more it makes sense. To have a life form dedicated to collecting conscious thought. It's how we are all connected to the universe. Our thinking is very powerful, we are what we think. Which also ties into what happens to us when we pass over. In the spirit world our thoughts become who we are. We manifest what we think. So if we think positive thoughts that's what we will experience. So you can see how much importance I place on positive thinking. Orbs are very much a real force in our lives; they are not paranormal, and as we evolve as spiritual beings we will become more and more aware of the different life forms we share our world and even our universe with. I'm very grateful to the orbs that allowed me to see them, they opened up a whole new train of thought for me, if you follow my way of thinking.

Although Ghost-house was a very serious place from time to time things happened that could be very amusing.

On one occasion the owners of Ghost-house invited a guest medium. I knew nothing about him, which would always make me very wary. I have worked with some very ego based mediums in the past, but I would always make them very welcome. I would arrive early and give them a tour round the house so they wouldn't get lost later in the evening, (believe me you could easily lose your bearings when it got dark.) This would also give them a chance to sense the feel of the house, again not always an easy thing to do when you have a crowd of forty people taking photo's asking questions, etc. It can be very intense. So I showed this medium round, let him do the talking so as not to give anything away. When we reached 'The Bishop's' room he happened to mention he was a trance medium. (This is a medium who allows spirits to enter their bodies, giving over all control to that spirit) Requesting that during that night's séance he would like to go into trance, assuring me that he had done this many times before. I had no reason to doubt him. But I knew he would be doing this in front of an audience of up to 50 people, so I agreed knowing that if anything went wrong I could rescue the situation. How wrong was I?

The evening progressed well with an above average crowd of enthusiastic people, eager to explore the house and its contents. Plenty happening; the house as always was very active, then the highlight of the evening - a séance conducted in 'The Bishop's' room dead on the stroke of midnight. Four of us sat down around the old oak table. Myself, two friends (who had done this a hundred times before) and our guest trance medium. I began "PLEASE USE OUR ENERGY TO COME THROUGH TO US." It would normally take a few minutes for messages to start coming in, but before I could open my mouth to ask spirit again to join us, our trance medium friend started rolling his eyes, swaying from side to side, then humming. This went on for about two minutes. I can honestly say that I have never ever seen anything like it. Then without any warning, (taking into consideration that the whole room was only lit by a few candles, everyone was watching in silence, the tension was so thick you could smell the anticipation in the cold damp air.) Both of his hands came down on the solid oak table with an almighty "THUMP!" Scared me witless. I had to check my trousers very quickly just to make sure! Then all I heard was this mediums voice saying in a very low tone "how long was l under"? Well this just made me burst out laughing. I know it wasn't very professional, but at that moment I had lost any sense of caring. This was the funniest thing I had ever seen during years of organizing séances. He really was good, that is good at playing us all along, then scaring the life out of the people watching, including me. By now the whole room had checked their own underwear, and was laughing along with my two friends and myself. Then without thinking about it I stood up and without thinking said "That's a demonstration on how **not** to hold a séance! If you ever see anything like this again please walk away!" The room just erupted in laughter. I managed to usher our guest medium out of the room and into the arms of the house owners, giving them a brief resume of what had happened. Needless to say I didn't see him again. Two good things came from this experience. The séance we held that night was the best ever, it was amazing, and everybody in that room was as one. Nothing like a near death experience to bring people together!

I also learned never to trust what people tell me about themselves. Another valuable lesson from spirit.

Just a little side line from that evening. The next morning, whilst getting ready to leave. I came across a group of middle aged ladies waiting in the lobby. This was the first time during the event these ladies had spoken to me. "Excuse me" said the tall blonde, "you're Dominic aren't you"? Well I had to agree I was Dominic! She went on "so pleased we caught you, last night was amazing we all enjoyed ourselves". "Thank you" I said a little embarrassed. I have never been able to take praise very easily, I'm told it's a childhood thing. Anyway she went on " we do lots of these ghost tours and see loads of mediums" I nodded in acknowledgement, "your guest medium" she went on "we saw him do the same thing during a séance last month, we were the only people in the room who were prepared, we knew what was coming". The other four ladies now listening to the conversation nodded as if one. "We all thought you handled the situation brilliantly" again l nodded and thanked her for her praise. She went on "I work for the local paper; it's not that big but would you do an interview for us about your work here at Ghost-house, it would be of great interest locally?" "Love too." I said without thinking. So the next morning I talked to the blonde lady on the phone about Ghost-house, its aims, and the spirits that reside there. The article was published and demand for tickets went through the roof. We couldn't keep up with the amount of enquirers. I have always thought spirit work in some strange ways. Small miracles happen every day. But if we hadn't invited that certain 'guest medium' Ghost-house wouldn't have reached the number of people it did. Good comes out of everything we do as long as we keep a positive attitude.

Ghost-house was sold in the spring of 2005. It now belongs to a new family who have restored the tired building back to its old former Glory.

I know the spirits that reside there will be happy to see their house being used as a family home once again.

As for me, I had four years of exploring a place few will ever get to explore. I feel honored to have been a part of something that taught me and others so much about the side of life we would all want to know about.

One day I would like to go back, just to see if 'The Bishop' was still in his room; I'm sure nothing would have changed.

Moving On

Time goes by so fast, the seasons come and go as one year fades into the next, so if a chance comes by to take a break I'm more than happy to go with it. But were does a medium go for a break? I have voices in my head 24 hours a day so you never really get away from spirit, even though I don't mind admitting it would be nice just for a day not to have the sound of spirit bouncing around my mind. In the back of my mind I remembered a place in North Wales. The Skirrid Inn. One of the most haunted places I had ever visited.

How good would it be to go back some five years later not for work but for pleasure?

My life had changed so much since I was last there. My dad had taught me that life as a mortal was far too short to be unhappy. Not by anything he had said, but by his lack of choice towards the end of his life through his illness.

He had to stay with my mother, however given the choice would prefer to have left.

My mother was one very difficult person.

So as I approached the same age as my father was before he passed over I knew it was wrong for me not to make the right choice for myself. This wasn't easy, however I realised I at least had the choice.

So life had moved on. I had met a wonderful person who had come into my life almost by accident.

Needless to say spirit work in strange ways. So here I was on this summer's morning, packing up the car for a few days in Wales with my new partner and wife to be Alison.

The Journey

This is how I remember feeling as a child, the anticipation of what was to come. My memories of the Skirrid Inn where vast. One of the most haunted buildings with the exception of Ghost-house I had ever stayed in. The Inn wasn't that big. It had become a modern public house with a friendly bar and restaurant down stairs, but it was upstairs that I remember with a mixture of excitement and fear. I knew Alison had never been in a haunted house, (well, not a real one) so the experience for her was going to be just a little scary mixed with amazement.

I was looking forward to spending time back in the place where I had first experienced a very special type of ghost.

'A shadow ghost'. This is the negative energy left from a person's soul when the soul transcends to the spirit dimension. The heavier negative energy splits from the soul and remains Earth bound as an energy in its own right.

This type of ghost is very rare, in over 40 years of exploring old buildings I have only ever come across a shadow ghost twice.

The Skirrid Inn and Ghost-house

When I first visited the Skirrid Inn (some years before) I was with a group of keen ghost seekers. They really wanted to discover "The Truth." I'm always a little reticent to get involved with such groups.

I'm not one for finding reasons to believe 'knocks and bangs' with people calling out "is anything out there wanting to make contact, let yourself be known to us".

To me that is nonsense. Let's get real and explore, only looking for the personal experience that can prove 'beyond doubt' something which we haven't yet come to understand is happening.

My first indication of a shadow ghost being present was by sight. It was one of the ladies in the group. For no apparent reason just breaking down, sobbing uncontrollably.

She just couldn't help herself.

The Shadow ghost had past right through her as she entered the room.

No warning or sense, just total emotional overload.

As I approached to comfort her I saw what could only be described as a black dust cloud the size of a small pillowcase rush past me and disappear into the corner of the room.

Even years later it still sends shivers down my spine just recalling the events of that evening.

Now all those years later my thoughts went back to the first time I had stayed. I could not help wonder what new experiences Alison and I might share this time? Would the shadow ghost still be in the corner of the room where I last saw it first time round?

The history of the Skirrid Inn is very interesting. It's an 11 century Inn.

The oldest inn still standing in Wales.

The upstairs was used as a court house where Judge Jeffries presided over trials of those who had been accused of crimes such as sheep rustling. The sentence would be death by hanging, which would take place almost as soon as sentence had been passed. A reminder of this was the noose that still hung from the top of the celling, dropping down through the wooden stair well. Over a hundred men had met their fate in that stairwell. No wonder the energy of all those souls was still left inside the four walls of the Inn.

So as we drove through the small roads over the Welsh hills my mind went back to the events of the past. I just couldn't stop myself thinking what The Skirrid Inn might have in store for the two of us this time. It wasn't going to let me down.

Arrival

Turning the corner there it was, not that impressive from the outside. A stone fronted building with wooden tables lined up at the front next to the road.

A small concealed entrance by the side of the inn lead to a rather large car park and gardens at the back.

Parking the car we both stood back to allow Alison to take her first glimpse of the old building.

Stone in construction with small windows jutting up through the slate roof. It was old but time hadn't aged the outside. The people who had cared for this lovely old house had more than looked after it.

With a glance at each other (the sort of look children give just before entering into a den), we walked through the open gate and rang the bell, no answer; so me being me I just opened the small green wooden door.

It was just how I remembered. In fact it was like walking back in time; nothing had changed in the years I had been away. The new owner, a rather large man with a bright red face and short cropped hair welcomed us in his soft Welsh voice. I expected a loud booming voice (people always surprise me when the voice doesn't fit the body.)

We were in luck. We had the whole upstairs all to ourselves. The landlord was very happy to let us have all the keys to the three main upstairs rooms.

This was far more than I could have hoped for, not only would we be sleeping here for three nights we could explore each and every square inch. Perfect.

The three rooms were all different. As we walked up the old wooden staircase with the noose hanging above our heads, just swaying gently in the light breeze.

At the top of the staircase there was a small landing with three large black doors all fitted with modern day Yale locks. I could remember from before that the door to the right was the old courtroom, which was the room with the shadow ghost. No way was I sleeping in that room!

The far right room was small, just about room for one. So the room on the left was the only option.

Turning the key we pushed open the heavy door to be met by bright midday sunshine coming in through a large window, directly to our right.

The room was very large. The size of a modern living room. A grand four poster bed at one end with a sofa and two easy chairs at the other. Then there was an open door going down to a sunken bathroom via a small staircase and safety rail. The bathroom was a room about 12 foot square with a wicker butterfly chair at one end and a large dark wooden beam crossing the shallow celling from left to right. The bath was situated just to one side of the beam. The toilet and small sink located in the far right corner. Almost as soon as I stood at the top of the staircase I could feel this was a very active part of the room. What I would later come to realise was the right hand corner of the bathroom was in the past a part of the room prisoners would be locked in before execution. The condemned cell.

Behind the wall where the toilet was located was now a store cupboard which was the old entrance to the cell. This area was very active. It had an uneasy feel, which is no surprise; after all it would echo with the last moments of fear before the person was taken out to the stair well then had the noose placed over their head and dropped to their death, down the narrow gap between the stairs. Without exaggeration you could sense the fear.

Alison was by now very excited. Whether she could feel the energy or not, she wanted to take the dowsing rods and see what ghostly force she could pick up.

Dowsing rods are a very simple way of experiencing spirit energy. Two metal rods about 30 centimetres in length bent about two thirds from the end at a 90 degree angle with plastic tubing so the rods could be held but would also swing free if in contact with spirit energy.

The person holding them could not affect the speed or the direction the rods would swing. I just knew that the bathroom would be the place to start exploring.

But first it was time to unpack and eat. The journey had been a long one and before we started to connect with the long lost souls of The Skirrid Inn, we had a few more human tasks to perform.

Orbs, rods and bras

The sun slid behind the slopping shoulders of the Skirrid Mountain, the black outline against an otherwise flat horizon. The moon hung in the sky directly above the mountain, like an invisible cord was holding it in exactly the right place. The view from the window was inspiring. Coming from Norfolk I rarely saw hills, let alone mountains.

Alison had a bath and laid all her clothes out for the next day carefully on the back of the wicker chair; jeans, tee shirt and bra, ready to put on the next morning. She climbed into bed and fell fast asleep (something about traveling long distance.)

Not a sound, apart from the occasional car driving past the front of the old inn.

Next morning the sun was up early, blue skies and a haunted building to explore.

Alison got out of bed and walked across to the stairs leading down to the bathroom. Her preparation the night before meant no thinking needed. A wash, straighten and brush her hair, get dressed and go down the stairs outside the room for breakfast.

I heard a scream! Alison had walked into the bathroom and instead of her clothes being neatly laid out on the chair, her bra was hanging from the smallest of black nails on the oak beam over the bath.

This beam was about seven foot off the ground which would have taken a ladder climb or stool just to reach the hook. The bra just hung, like it had always been there, just left hanging in midair.

Considering the history of the room, plus the fate that lay in wait for so many men (held in the cell at the back of the bathroom) I could not help but wonder were the ghosts of the inn showing us the fate that had befallen them using Alison's bra as an example?

This unnerved both of us. Yes I had encountered many different forms of ghostly energies, but I had never had any of my personal clothing moved and just left hanging. The strange thing was neither of us felt uncomfortable in the room. We had both slept soundly without as much as a dream.

The bra incident was something unexpected, caught me a little off guard. All my life I have watched as objects have appeared then disappeared, or been moved to a different location by spirit for a reason. This is 'teleportation'. The Victorian mediums would fake pennies falling from above the séance table, claiming the money was a gift from spirit. The noise of the coins would scare the on lookers and of course prove the existence of the realm of spirit. To modern day mediums this show of evidence was an obvious tick, but teleportation, or the moving of objects has been witnessed and filmed happening on camera, so there is something in it.

Last night it happened right in front of us both, I just hope the intention was not to scare, but to indicate that something or someone was trapped inside that sunken bathroom. I did not want to draw too many conclusions without investigating first. After all a bra hanging from a beam might relate to a person being hung, a symbol or demonstration of a cruel act that took place many centuries before in the same energy space. Or it could just be an act of mischief by the ghosts who want to remain in their current location?

Investigation

After breakfast, I decided to set up a few experiments in the bathroom. Alison had taken control of the dowsing rods which they were merrily swinging round in large circles. The indications were that most of the energy in this bathroom was still very active.

In locations like this I would set up my voice recorder, this would capture any 'EVP's' (Electronic Voice Phenomenon) Spirits have been known to leave voice messages on electronic devices such as televisions, computers or voice recorders. (I have touched on this subject in a previous chapter.) I would also set up some dusting experiments. By placing an object like a coin on a surface, table top, or window ledge you can see if spirit have moved its position. Like the bra being taken from the chair and hung on the old wooden beam.

All of my efforts went unrewarded, yes the dowsing rods would still fly around in Alison's hands in various locations. I captured some orbs on digital camera and a 'rod' not as common as orbs, just not as interesting. A 'rod' is a thin line of multi-coloured lights which move around a room in unnatural directions, jumping and jerking from one location to another at great speed.

I believe 'rods' are intelligent life, compressed into a pure form. This energy would travel vast distances across the universe, not being affected by time or distance. These energy driven life forms not dissimilar to the makeup of our soul energy.

All Good Things

Taking everything into consideration we both had an enjoyable stay. The Inn was very active, and the ghosts of the past still present. No shadow ghost this time though.

During our stay we had parked our car in the rear car park of the inn. This car park was right next door to the church yard. Some believe the church to be an active location. I still have my doubts about the church. However as we got to drive away I noticed that the paper tax disc which in those days would have to be displayed in the bottom left of the car's windscreen was missing!

Our car had not been out of the car park, locked at all times. So where was the tax disc?

For some reason unknown the disc had been taken out of its holder and placed in the passenger glove compartment! Obviously the ghosts of The Skirrid Inn had not wanted us to leave without saying goodbye.

Paranoid or?

Most of us go through the same experiences. Yes in our own way, but whatever you are going through someone before you has trodden the same path.

Hard to relate to when it feels like you are the only person feeling the way you do.

When we talk about our own personal experiences, many would have had a different, but similar story to tell.

The problem with identifying this is we can only see something through our own personal eyes. Never easy to 'suspend' your own experiences and listen without prejudice. Worth a try though, you never know what you may have missed, and another may have learnt.

CHAPTER FIVE

More to Heaven and Earth

I am not a person who stays in touch, Christmas cards and social media are enough for me. I have always made time for people. My phone can go and I will make time to speak with or help, if possible. Over the years I have discovered that people know where I am if needed, but often after everything has settled back down I seldom hear. I fully understand this and welcome the quiet moments.

There are a few exceptions to this, Hazel, Victor and Burt.

Hazel and Vic have been married for over sixty years, having met before the Second World War then spending the entire war apart. Victor an officer in the Army. Vic would not talk about his war time service but I have it on good authority he was on the beaches at Dunkirk, then back again for the invasion of Europe, before that Italy then Africa. Hazel's war was spent working on the farms of south east England. She had been a land girl. Burt, Hazels elder brother had sailed the world in the merchant Navy. Together they had gone through many stressful situations. Very impressive people.

I met Hazel shortly after her brother Burt passed. In his later life Burt became a very popular, sort after spiritual healer. Hazel would tell me stories of how Burt would sit crossed legged on the floor next to his Indian guides, chatting away in his own language. The atmosphere would be thick with pipe smoke as the conversations would go on for hours.

I know how close they were as siblings, both looking out for each other.

Hazel was left heart broken when at the age of eighty six Burt crossed over after a short illness.

As a medium Burt made it very easy for me to connect to him for his sister. Hazel appreciated my honest and straight forward approach to mediumship. I have always stuck carefully to the messages doing my best to repeat them word for word. Only on the odd occasion changing the wording to save embarrassment. (I will tell you the story of the hen pecked man at the end of this chapter.)

When Burt first came through to me the message was full of evidence of survival. He had agreed with Hazel and Vic to say a few special words through a medium, I was the first medium to repeat these words.

As a medium I would fully recommend agreeing upon a sentence or a group of words before you pass, with your loved ones, this makes my job so much easier. I have learnt that working as a medium comes with a high price, many are sceptical and rightly so. Being able to bring through random words that have meaning leave little doubt and is the best evidence.

Both had vast experience working with the spiritual church and healing. They knew what needed to be done. After that moment Hazel and Vic became firm friends, I would go as far as saying they both became mentors to me. I missed (with no parental interest) having people to discuss things with. Hazel and Vic were always there for me, I grew to love them both very much.

Iron Cross

So you can imagine how I felt the morning when my phone rang and Hazel's anxious voice was on the other end.

"You have to help me" Well it went without saying that I would do anything for Hazel but first I had to know what it was that had concerned her so much.

This is what happened next.

When Burt had passed over to spirit he had left very little behind. He was not a person to gather possessions, he had lived a simple life without need.

The one item he had treasured was an iron cross he wore around his neck, (he'd had it for as far back as Hazel could remember.) This cross was the one thing Hazel had to remind her of Burt.

Every day she would carefully place her brother's cross around her neck, taking it off only to go to bed at night. The cross would be laid next to her clock on the bedside table. Same routine every day.

This particular morning Hazel had woken, went to put the cross on, and it had vanished. Nowhere to be seen, she had checked all the likely places, under the bed, in the toilet, next to her chair in the sitting room. No sign.

The phone call was then made, Hazel asked me if I could contact Burt and ask him directly; she was sure if this iron cross was to be found it would be her brother Burt who would know.

Calming Hazel down I promised I would ask Burt for her. I did not expect what happened next.

Burt had always been a cheerful man; a bright welcome, soft voice. The one person he cared for was Hazel.

I did not have to work that hard to create the link. Burt was waiting.

Yes he had moved the iron cross from his sister's bedside table, but he had done it for a reason.

Hazel was a long time diabetic, she had managed her condition for years. At times of stress, or moments when life got too much she would lapse and give in to her weakness - chocolate.

Vic knew her only too well and would keep an eye on his wife, he knew that Hazel was capable of hiding Mars bars, or Smarties and disappearing on her own to tuck in. This was very bad, Hazel's blood sugars could shoot up and send her into a coma. Burt knew this.

He told me that the only way he could stop his sister eating Smarties was to move the iron cross right next to where she had hidden them. He knew she would miss the cross, then the likelihood would be she would get in touch with me and I could tell Vic what Hazel had been up to.

Hazel had been eating Smarties hidden in the bathroom cabinet. The one place where she could go in the house without being questioned.

The iron cross was in that cabinet right next to the sweets. He made me promise to tell Vic before Hazel.

I was relieved the cross had been found, or should I say located, but the problem of telling Vic remained. Difficult to phone Vic without Hazel knowing.

So I phoned and Hazel answered the phone, as usual. I asked if Vic was in the room and requested that they both listened in to what I had to say.

I could hear the echo of my voice as the phone was switched over to loudspeaker.

"Hazel I have located your brother's iron cross" I started. "It is in the bathroom cabinet, right next to that tube of Smarties which you have been eating!" I heard the living room door squeak open, Hazels footsteps, then her voice shouting "Got it!" The relief in her voice audible across the hall way.

All Vic could do was laugh, he knew what his wife was like, but he never knew that Burt would still be able to intervene.

Hazel was caught red handed, with her fingers in the Smarties. And she knew it. No hiding place would be safe from Burt, she laughed more in embarrassment and relief than anything else.

Her sweet hiding days were well and truly over.

Hazel and Vic lived well into their nineties, both passing over within three months of each other, first Vic and then Hazel. By the time Hazel stepped across she had dumfounded doctors by her fighting spirit. Most people would have gone over years before. Hazel never did want to be parted from Victor; childhood sweethearts, who together had gone through so much. When Vic went, Hazel lost the will to fight on.

I still miss my friends. Not a day goes by when something happens or I am working (helping people come to terms with losing a loved one) that I do not think of them. I know they are often with me, watching to make sure I keep up the standards required to connect the two sides of life.

"So much more to living than life" Hazel would say this to me often, and although in my early thirties I sort of got what she meant. I get it so much more now in my mid-fifties. I still question and I still want to know 'how and why' but I am so much more accepting. There is so much which we do not know or cannot explain rationally, I just witness and accept.

The Henpecked man

Unexpected

The doorbell rang, my first client of the day had arrived, very early. I never minded, I would think back to the day's when I would turn up early for appointments, hoping to be able to talk first. This rarely happened and I would be left waiting in drafty hall ways, or worse, told to come back later. So on opening the door there stood in front of me a well-dressed lady, not a hair out of place, makeup skillfully applied.

As I do for anyone who comes to sit with me I put the kettle on and offer a drink. This lady was having none of that. She wanted to get on with the reading. She was easily over twenty five minutes early but I could feel her not wanting to engage in small talk.

So we sat down in my living room, not the normal room I read in.

She looked me directly in the eyes and said, "Tell me why I have come to see you"? Most clients are not that direct, they have been through loss of some kind, but most are happy to allow the sitting to unfold gently. Not this lady. She wanted answers fast.

Everything was to become clear.

In mind sight came a man, he told me his name, and a little about the sudden heart attack that had taken him over extremely fast. No time to prepare, no illness, just one minute eating dinner, the next in spirit. He told me that the lady with the impatient manner was his wife of twenty five years. And although she had been a good wife to him and mother to their children she had never let him out of her sight. She had made his life a misery, controlling everything from what he wore, to the food he would eat.

This explained the toga he was wearing and the rather large glass of red wine he was holding! Now I am open to anything, spirit have taught me not to judge, but I just knew this man had been henpecked all of his married life and was so relieved to get away from his domineering partner.

So picture the scene, here I am in my own living room, an anxious and over baring lady making demands, with her late husband in spirit, enjoying a glass of wine, at a toga party which his relatives were holding for him! I could not tell this women he was so pleased to be away from her, could I? The truth on this occasion would be hurtful, it certainly would not be welcome. For the first time I had to make up a different message, it went something like this; - "I have your husband here, he past suddenly of a heart attack and his name was David. He wants to say thank you for all the years you looked after him and making sure he had a life where he needed for nothing. He adds he loves you very much. (What he had really said, and please forgive me, was; Oh no, she has followed me again! Why can't she just let go and leave me in peace!)

Tears

Message relayed and understood. The lady burst into tears. I have seen this many times but each time it happens I hate it. I can deal with smiles, but tears leave me not always knowing how to react.

She was happy, my work was done. Her husband had given her the evidence she needed, without upsetting her further.

I rarely meet people like this, most that call are lovely. The responsibility is a heavy one and not something I take lightly. But it is also important to keep a sense of reality. I do not meet people when they are happy. Being a medium is not something I would choose to be.

I have learnt to expect the unexpected. Every single day I work I have always felt nervous before I start, then once working I do not have time to think about nerves.

From the moment I start to the waving goodbye at the end of the last private sitting, time has no meaning.

I can be placed in all sorts of dilemmas. I meet so many different people; from the regal and famous, then to the lady who lives all alone in a small flat. Each person gets my undivided attention no matter what. Not everyone I meet is happy to see me, sceptics, and doubters, even those who are so conditioned by fear. I feel their hostility long before I say anything. Not everyone is nice. Including those who work for the church, or those who work for large media organisations.

In this age of equality for all, mediums are not included.

Stopping

Do you ever stop and think about how others may see you? The effect we have on those around us can be far more profound than we know. I believe we rarely come to realise the good, often preferring to focus on the bad. 'Too bossy', too opinionated, too quick to anger, or judge. We seldom see the good, before the difficult. So who are the 'safe' people in your life? The ones you can say anything too, without them reacting? These are the people we must stop and think about first. The ones who do not react or judge us. They just accept us, choose to share with us, whilst understanding our moods and behaviour.

The safe people in our lives are often forgotten because they are always there.

CHAPTER SIX

Alien Life

So much of my life has been exploration. Yes as a child I would love to play football, like any other young child I never gave any thought to what I was doing.

Days were long and worries few.

Life is simple through the eyes of a child, only adults complicate and confuse.

My younger version of the universe was much as it is today, I have never shifted my opinions on the likelihood of intelligent life being common place. My personal love for knowledge knew no bounds. I would visit second hand book shops looking for anything on UFO's. Adult books sharing stores of 'Men in Black' or flying discs which would fly at tremendous speeds. To my young mind it made sense that aliens would be visiting, the stories of people like Betty and Barney Hill the first people in America to claim to have been abducted by aliens would only go on to fuel my already active imagination.

Being a child is never easy, any opinions or knowledge which you may have can easily be dismissed as fantasy.

However my interested never died, it just grew. I had a thirst for knowledge, and a keen eye for detail.

I believe in personal experience; we can read as many books or listen to accounts, but these are just someone else's versions.

In this next chapter I would like to explain a few things I have come to understand.

All views are my own.

How to meet an Alien

The world is full of wonder, much of which we miss. The more free time we are given the more we speed up. Life is lived at a hundred miles an hour. No time to stop or consider.

We live in big cities, with mass crowds of other people who remain strangers, even though we sit next to them on the buses and trains. Preferring to keep our eyes down, hiding behind mobile phones and newspapers which tell us nothing.

The world has become a place to hide in, a place not to notice.

It may be no coincidence that the more we camouflaged ourselves, the more we strive to be noticed, displaying photographs and personal details on social media.

At this moment in history the world we live in and amongst is a world full of paradoxes.

Personal Reality

Our own beliefs are at the centre of who we are. These beliefs are built up over many years of personal experiences, self-taught knowledge, but by far the strongest influence over what we come to believe in are our senses. Long before we talk, or express our opinions we sense them. If something feels right we will tell ourselves it often is. But just to get to adulthood we have had to go through much in the way of teaching. We are taught what to think from an early age. Religion forms a vast amount of this. Our young minds are susceptible to suggestion.

As we get older our belief structures become more cemented in our personality and much more unlikely to be altered, the exception to this is 'personal experience'. Personal experiences will change what we come to believe in. But (and it is a large but) when we have a deeply held belief we will not seek alternatives; even if they are right in front of us, the invisible will remain invisible because we will not choose to see or acknowledge. If we do not believe, we will not seek. In our opinion there is nothing to seek.

Open Mind

Our personal picture of the world is based on these three foundations. What we are taught, what we adopt as our own, and personal experiences, which teach us something different. If we are wise we will explore the possibilities, keeping an open mind and seeking answers. Molding the information into who we become. In short, believing makes exploration possible.

The Universe

Beyond imagination. We cannot even start to understand the numbers, distance and complexion of the universe. Even if we narrow the universe down to just our galaxy, the number of stars are still beyond our comprehension. And although we have opened the door to space travel, we still have not come to terms with the 'time verses distance' equation. We still think in light years, traveling vast distances across space, is as perplexing to us as a box of matches would be to a stone age man.

Many would believe wrongly that if we cannot do it, then it cannot be done. This argument is at best naïve. History has shown otherwise. If we can think it we can do it. We just have to discover how. Traveling vast distances across space will happen, it is just a case of when, not if.

Alien Life

Now you do not have to suspend your own personal beliefs, you just have to look at the numbers and put all the pieces together. Earth like planets are not that rare. The Hubble space telescope has taught us this. The maths is astonishing, just in our galaxy we could be looking at millions of Earths. As incredible as this sounds you then have to multiply this figure by billions of galaxies. The numbers stack up and point to alien life being common place. Even if you factor in a percentage of alien civilizations not reaching space, there could be alien life so far advanced with technology we could not even imagine to be possible, the fact of their existence would remain invisible. So past our comprehension.

Believing in alien life is far easier than not believing. The argument that Earth is the only planet across a vast universe which has intelligent, evolved life just does not stand up. The maths shows us otherwise.

Alien Life on Earth

We now can see the possibilities, alien life exists. We can debate the numbers and the technical levels, but we can agree that the universe will be home to civilizations of evolved extra-terrestrial life. These beings could possess the technology to travel across vast distances. But why would they want to visit this planet? We have already stated that there are millions of Earth like planets in our own galaxy, why come to this hostile, primitive world?

It certainly would not be to dominate, or rule; this is far too human. Extra-terrestrials would have passed this phase of their evolution and survived to build space ships which explore, traveling to seek out new life. Sounds familiar, well it should 'Star Trek' was written by Gene Roddenberry in the nineteen sixties after he claimed he had experienced alien contact. Personal experience which changed Roddenberry's life. The invisible became visible.

Aliens have a need to explore, experience, even guide. Why would they not want to watch other civilizations evolve?

You could take this to another level and consider the possibilities that aliens choose to live amongst us.

Now this could extend your own personal belief structure far beyond your comfort zone, but why not explore this without judgement?

When we open our minds to the possibilities the invisible becomes visible. We might start to notice some of the characteristics of alien life, if we know what to look for. If I am right, aliens could be living in plain sight, mixing, traveling and exploring our planet right next to us on the train, or the bus, in the shopping malls and even in the centres of cultural understandings.

By being aware of what to look for, maybe you might have your own personal alien experience which could alter your own perception of the universe.

Types of Alien

Here are a few brief descriptions of aliens you may see mixing with the general population in plain sight.

The Tall White

Long slender arms and legs with albino white hair and skin colouring, and between 6 to 8 feet tall. These aliens will dress like us, often wear dark glasses but stand out because of their stature and physique. They are social and approachable but they do not like psychical contact. Their bodies are a lot less robust, taking a long time to heal if injured. They are the only aliens to travel with their children.

Places to see them. Shopping malls, casinos and public transport. They are often accompanied by their human hosts. So look for small groups of people with, one maybe two taller companions that are extremely thin with very blond hair.

Stocky 5' 6" Human looking Alien

These aliens are harder to spot. Often on their own, they blend into the crowd with ease. The signs to look for are: - no hair, eyebrows will be drawn or tattooed on to the fore brow. Short, stocky with square shaped head. Dark tanned skin. These aliens will avoid eye contact and are believed to be telepathic.

Likely to be seen on public transport and live in large cities where they can blend into the background. Their shape, size and lack of hair are all very noticeable if you know what you are looking for.

Just two examples of aliens who live amongst us in plain sight.

Our Planet

The world is a wondrous place, full of culture, language and art. We are so diverse yet similar. The Earth is a planet which holds much curiosity for any intelligent life to explore.

I have no doubt because of my own personal experiences that the universe is teaming with life. Life so diverse we could never imagine what is out there, just waiting for us to discover. Many are starting to agree with me, not because I want them too but because they are encountering, and having their own personal experiences.

Keep your thoughts open, and your mind engaged with knowledge, know what to look for and you too may have your own experience. You never know you may be sat on a train or bus right now next to a visitor from another planet.

Psychic

Psychic - now there's a word which has so many different meanings and purpose.
A person said to me yesterday - "I am a little bit psychic."
Well maybe we all are, 'a little bit'! Just depends on what we are doing at the time.
The thought we could all be anything is one of those things which once thought of grows into something completely different.
The version of who we are is only ours. Nobody really knows if what we say is real, or a figment of our imagining.
I could conclude that we are what we think we are. Even if that amounts to being a little bit of anything.

CHAPTER SEVEN

Psychic Understanding

Many of my best moments have been accompanied by music. Throughout my life music has followed me around. I can remember as a child, no more than eight years old, father pulling me to one side telling me to 'Let it be'. The lyrics from that famous song stuck inside my head, even now during 'times of troubles'.

As a medium music is an escape. I can play my favourite songs and move into the music as it penetrates my ears and pushes deep into my psyche. It drowns out the voices; the constant chatter which is always present in my head. I am not sure people realise how 'constant'.

On the plus side I am never alone. Voices will come out of the background, hum and engage me in conversation. A comparable is walking through a train station on a busy Friday afternoon. People and noise everywhere, the general din broken by the station announcer with the arrival times of the next trains. My head feels like that every day. Hard to understand when you do not have voices in the centre of your head.

I have never held the view that I'm lucky to hear voices. To me yes, it has its moments when you can prove survival beyond doubt to a grieving relative. Then there are times (no matter how hard you try) you cannot find the spirit person you need to find. The din becomes over whelming, the frustration immense. Again people do not understand the difficulty in making the exact contact. When a person comes to me they do not want to be connected to the whole family tree. Just the person they want to hear from. If that spirit person is nowhere to be heard from, or they give the wrong evidence, it can be awkward. Many expect miracles; most get what they want but a few do not. I have to remind them that I am a medium, I have no right to spirit contact.

The two worlds are completely different.

The world we inhabit (whilst mortal) is so different to the realm of spirit. Please do not get drawn into believing that the two worlds mirror each other, they do not. In this mortal world we have to think first, then act, then wait. And after all this we still may not achieve. Our will has to be strong, focused. Mortal living is just that, everything has a time life, everything is achievable. We have to understand what it is we are wanting.

Some mediums mix up the two sides of life. They claim that we grow old in spirit; this in my opinion is wrong. When we pass back to the realm of spirit the life time just left finishes there. Our consciousness is then added to the consciousness of all our previous life times. One ball of cosmic energy, comprising of all the identities we have ever been. This is our soul. No time in spirit, no one identity.

If you come to me for a private sitting and you want your father to come through, your thoughts have to mirror this. Remember the man you knew as your father is likely to have had many different life times as many different people. If I do not connect to him in spirit as the man you knew then the evidence is going to be wrong.

I have discovered that if a person is emotionally upset, or difficult, demanding or even disbelieving, it makes my task so much more difficult. This is why I believe that 'love' is the only truth in the universe. When a person comes with love, and genuine reasons to reconnect the connections always happen. The soul reacts to love, the energy is then uncomplicated, allowing the energy from the section of the soul you want to reach to come through.

From personal experience this happens time after time.

It is worth remembering that we do not grow old in spirit. So the next time you hear a medium talk about little Johnny who passed when he was an infant, and now is a grown man in spirit think why?

Manifestation

I will often joke with my clients that being impatient is to be spiritual. I truly believe this.

The closer we are to the universe the more we want to manifest.

The realm of spirit is thought energy based. Whatever we can think we can manifest. So whilst in spirit out thoughts become things. That which we have stored in our soul memory can be recreated.

This mortal world is purely for the purpose of creating memories and experiences. The two different dimensions work hand in hand. Be careful what you come to believe in, because this will be the reality you create when you move over. The realm of spirit means something different to each and every one of us.

Knowing this helps so much when it comes to wanting to connect with your own spirit guides, mentors and past self; soul memory.
Put yourself in the position of 'spirit', and the rest will fall into place.

Guided Meditation

One of my favourite meditations is the one I have been doing since I was about fourteen. Before I go on to describe it to you there are a few things that you should be aware of.

Your senses are key. Everything you experience as a mortal are locked inside your five senses.

Use them.

Being in spirit is about recall. What it feels like to taste, touch, see, hear and smell. All of these can be recreated either in your thoughts or by the inclusion of scent.

All senses are equally as important. Visitation is based on inner calm, and a peaceful mind. You can take yourself anywhere if you have the right environment.

Smell is something that can transport you to anywhere you want to be in an instant. It is the first sense you come to use when first born. Find the smells that suit you and your meditation.

Taste is the next sense, just before sound. Learn to recognise the different tastes. Without sight taste is more difficult than you may think. Try it, describe different flavours whilst blindfolded.

Sound. Learn to hear what makes up the sound. A good exercise is to put your favourite piece of music on and only listen for one component part of the music. Isolate the piano, or the drums and just listen to that one section. You will hear so much more. Most of what we hear is only a fraction of what we could be listening too.

Now you have the idea follow my lead and try this.

The Tree

Visualise yourself in a meadow, the grass is long and damp, touching your ankles, cold against your skin. In the distance you can hear a blackbird, singing loudly above all the other birds. The sun is warm against your shoulders and you shield your eyes against the glow, the smell of the nearby woodlands fills your nostrils with scent.

As you walk along the grassy path twigs snap under your feet, the sound rings in your ears, you stop to pick a ripe blackberry, the taste; Sharpe on your tongue, the pips annoying as they stick in your teeth.

Ahead you notice an old oak tree, just standing regal in amongst smaller younger trees.

Taking a closer look you notice in the trunk an old wooden door. The metal hinges rusted into the wood, the old black cold iron door knob smooth as you reach out to turn the handle.

The door opens with a squeak, you peer inside, the smell of the moss and damp wood fills your senses as your eyes adjust to the dim light.

You can just make out a pin prick of light coming from the very top of the hollowed out tree. A stone staircase winds its way up and around in a spiral, disappearing from view then coming back into sight as the steps become narrow.

Intrigued, you start to climb. You can hear the sound of water dropping onto the stone; the smell of the moss mixed with the wood grows even stronger as you climb. The thin crack of light around the door fades as your feet stretch higher on the cold grey stone stairs. Your hands brush against the damp wood, and little pieces break off and feel brittle between your finger and thumb as they crumble into dust.

The light now shines in through the round hole in the top of the trunk. Warm and welcoming you feel compelled to keep climbing towards the ever growing gap in the wood. As you reach the exit your eyes meet an emerald green carpet of lush green grass, sprinkled with golden heads of yellow dandelions. You can smell the fresh bright air, the birds singing and the insects dancing, butterflies drift past on the gentle breeze. You choose to sit under an old apple tree, first reaching out and snapping a red ripe apple from its branches, before tasting the sweet crisp creamy white tangy fruit. You close your eyes are settle down under the warm sun and light breeze to rest.

This is now your place, a place that no one, only you knows about; a place so secret it only exists because of you. This will be where you come to talk with you guides, angels and mentors.

Once you have your own special place build on it. Make it uniquely yours.

This is your first step, ask your inner self what you want to understand from being here. What answers are you seeking? Remember all the knowledge we may ever need is locked inside, we just need to know where to look.

I have written this meditation out in full and you will find it at the end of this book.

Looking for Clues

Every single person I have met would like to have the ability to know the future. In many areas of our everyday life we come across situations which need us to make choices or decisions. Being alive is a mixture of choice coupled with both finding our own purpose and decision making. Knowing what the outcome is going to be, no matter what we decide is the key to making the right choices. But what if there was no wrong choice? Apart from making no choice. Wouldn't that make life easier? Or would the time we took to achieve be how we judged ourselves? Considering time as a circle would set us free. Whichever direction we set out in we would always reach the same point, it would just take us longer depending on the direction we travel on in the first place, and how long it takes us to decide to start walking.

To play the game we must at first throw the dice.

Establishing our life path is not as hard as it seems. Especially if we have had the same life many times before. Like playing a board game, the more familiar we become with the 'consequence' of making the wrong moves the easier it becomes to make better choices. On a board game we can clearly see ahead, what our end objective is. Life is a little more complex. But the more we discover our 'end goal' the easier getting there becomes.

This is where we can gain an advantage by understanding we have lived the same life over and over again. We would have made the wrong choices many times, our actions would have taken us into a Cul- de- sac which we had no way out of, but the more times we repeat the same actions with the same consequence the more familiar these choices become, the more we will recognise we are making the wrong decisions; our inner self or voice will be shouting at us really loudly. If we learn to read the 'signs' correctly and listen we would always choose the best direction, it's only when we ignore the "inner voice" we all possess, we then face trouble, or find a block which slows us down or stops us in our tracks.

So how do we learn how to spot the 'signs'?

I hope that in the remainder of this book I can give you the clues to look out for. The things you may never have considered, the areas in which to search and of course the 'signs' to be on the lookout for.

First it is good to establish a way of thinking that will guide you into following my train of thought.

Who are we? Are we the sum total mass of the thoughts, beliefs and past actions we have accumulated during our life time? Or are we all of the above over many past life times? Or are we everything we are ever going to be with all our future actions submerged into the one relevant life, the current one?

It's true we can only ever be in one place at one time. The life we are leading has all the information stored relating to all of our past and future life times. This is called 'Cell Memory' which I will explain in further depth later in this chapter. For the moment you will just have to take my word for it. But the concept is real enough. Learning more about the inner workings of the soul will also help in finding clues to the direction of your current life.

Psychic Development

You can spend your money on so many different psychic development aids. Packs of Tarot or Angel cards, books and teaching on 'how to' so many confusing and conflicting methods to choose from. All have their merits and only one flaw, they are how somebody else would do it; not how you would.

I have heard the same words from different people so many times - "I just don't know how to hear spirit." Most get some way to understanding how to; breathe, relax, meditate etc. but get stuck when these teachings don't bring many spiritual benefits.

I see the same teachings recycled by different teachers. Nothing new, nothing which points the individual into using the one thing different for all of us - our senses.

I am reminded of a quote "The harder I work the luckier I get". This applies to spiritual development in so many ways. First not many want to work that hard, all will say they do, most will use the term 'I'm trying' some will buy all the gear and have no idea! But many stop when the going gets tough. Shifting from one concept to another, seeking out the latest 'teachers' without planning a direction.

Spirit are very simple, nothing complicated or difficult, the key to spiritual understanding is very straight forward.

Follow these main points:

1.   You must have an inner passion for what you want to do.
        (Without this 'passion' you will fail, because when you
        don't get results you will lose interest.)

83

2.   Prepare. Before you start anything in life the preparation
        is so very important. The preparation in this instance is all
        about how you feel and think. Your emotions must be in
        the right place; any emotional fears or problems must be
        cleared first. Your diet has to be aligned to you, being in
        the best possible shape both in mind and physically will
        give you the edge. So many try and develop without
        dealing with their life issues first.

3.   Do not set time limits. So many do. Try to think
        of learning without limits. Time should not come into your
        thoughts during your process along this path. (Time is just
        a human concept, no time in spirit just thought. We stop
        ourselves spiritually when we try to mix human values into
        spiritual knowledge.) Time brings pressure and
        expectations, both human traits. Thoughts become things,
        think spiritual, (become spiritual.)

So now you are ready to think the right thoughts. Your preparation
is done, mind and body are aligned and you have thrown away your human
way of thinking. Let's move on to some simple exercises that can help you
develop spiritually.

5 Senses

To work with yourself and yourself alone can be tough, no one to
give you short cuts or praise, just you. Think about this. You already have
in your 'cell memory' thousands of human life time experiences.

Your soul would have experienced much. You are your best
supporter, your best teacher, your best confidant. Everything you need to
succeed is already stored inside you. This is an important realisation. When
we reach out towards others for confirmation or praise it is because we are
not connecting to the 'inner self'. The 'Thought' self which we all are, when
in 'spirit'.

Learning about the 'human' senses.

CHAPTER EIGHT

Finding missing People, Animals and Objects

Missing

I cannot claim to be 'the first' in many things, however I was the first psychic in England to help people find missing objects, then missing animals and then help locate missing people. Like all good things it started by accident.

A lady had made a visit to see me from Scotland; a long way to come all the way to Norfolk. After the reading was over she casually threw into the conversation that the week before she had lost a seven thousand pound diamond earring. She had looked everywhere and had consigned herself to having lost it.

I have always held a keen interest in teleportation, (spirit moving objects by thought) I had come across some really good examples and thought that as a medium I could use the link or the 'vibration to spirit' to locate such missing items. After all, the main purpose of moving objects was for spirit to draw attention to themselves. What better way to get a loved one to contact somebody like me who worked with spirit energy?

So when this lady asked me about her diamond earring it felt natural to ask my voices.

On this occasion I was shown a black felt bag, with a cord and a small white label stitched into the side seem.

This lady looked at me with a puzzled sideways glance, "that is the little pouch they came in" she said without a second thought. The lady left and I thought no more of it.

The next day my office phone rings and it is the same lady. I am always pleased to hear from people who have come for readings, nice to be told how much the sitting has helped them.

Her voice was excited, she could hardly say hello. "You will never guess, what I found when I got home?" "My earring!" "It was in the little black bag just how you described."

I was not surprised, I was pleased for her, but like I said I know how spirit can play games with objects.

She went on; "the strange thing is I had turned that bag inside out the day before I left to see you, I would swear that the earring was not there then."

I explained a little about how every single object had a unique energy signature, that spirit will move items to get attention, and it was very likely that her diamond was teleported into spirit and back again.

She was delighted, overwhelmed by her experience. A miracle? Maybe. But spirit will move objects.

This one event then cascaded into many phone calls. Word of mouth is the best form of recommendation. Once people remark or talk about you, the phone never stops.

Wooden Box

Shortly after finding the earring I received a phone call from another lady. Her voice was anxious, she told me she had just left the hospital where her father had just passed. This is such a stressful time I will seldom read for those going through bereavement. It is tough enough losing a loved one, the last thing you should be thinking of is having a mediumship sitting.

So I was just about to say it was a little too soon to speak with me, when she said, "you are the medium who locates missing objects aren't you?" Yes it was true, I had found the diamond earring, and yes I did have an interest in teleportation. She continued, "I need your help, you see we cannot find the will, we know dad wrote one but he was very secretive about everything, he never shared where anything was." "Do you think you could contact dad and ask him?"

No problem in trying, I thought. So there and then whilst the lady was still on the phone I asked spirit. Now as I have explained in earlier chapters not every time I ask I receive help, it can take a while to connect to the right energy. Not this time. The man was already front and centre in mind sight. Grumpy old man with string holding up his brown trousers! No manners. I described him first, the lady (his daughter) almost dropped the phone! She had not expected contact. (I am sure people just clutch at straws and only turn to psychics through desperation, they seldom believe it is possible.)

This man went on to describe a cupboard under the stairs, a shelf, and a wooden box with a false lid. He told me that the lid had to be slid then twisted to reveal a secret compartment. Inside the compartment was the document - his will.

I could sense the lady not being too sure about the information. You get the feeling when someone is just going along with the moment. Yes she was happy about the description of her father, but she had never seen a wooden box on a shelf in the cupboard under the stairs. She promised the next day to take a look, and thanked me for my time! No word of, "how much do I owe you?" Mediums are supposed to give their time for free! After all it is a natural gift.

Sure enough the next day my phone rang, and it was this lady.

She could hardly get her words out quickly enough, "thank you so much!" "We have found the will exactly where you explained it would be!" "It's a miracle!" "How did you know?"

I explained a little about how mediumship worked, and just spoke about intent. "If spirit have the intent to help they will" I explained. "It can happen that people do not expect to pass over, they have made no preparation or left no instructions." Being a medium does have its benefits at times like these.

I never ever heard from that lady again. She never asked me if she could do anything for me, or even pay me for my time. I am sure people do not stop to think, too wrapped up in their own lives.

Finding lost objects is something I can do, but I never expected to be looking for missing animals and then people.

Mr. Green

Mr. Green is a rather large black and white tom cat. As all cats are, a dearly loved family pet. So when he went missing the owners Racheal, and her mother Linda soon found me.

Finding living animals is not that easy, but I have a method which has proved very successful. I use photographs.

When a photograph is taken the picture does not only capture the image, it also captures the energy, or the aura of the animal. (The Australian Aboriginals believe that when a photograph is taken of them, the taker steals a piece of their soul.) I believe the aura is captured and is an indication of whether the animal is still alive. The energy fades on photographs when a living creature dies.

So when someone asks me to look for a missing pet the first thing I do is ask for a recent photograph. This photograph determines whether or not I should search or not. Animals will go off on their own to die, especially dogs, they seem to be aware when their life is coming to an end. Just as people dying is private and personal; passing over to the realm of spirit is something animals like to do in private.

Once I have established the pet has not passed I arrange a personal visit to retrace the animals tracks, or as I have come to understand it as their energy signature. We all leave this energy behind us as we go about our daily routines, cats are no exception.

Picking up the unique energy signature is a simple task of picking up something like bedding, or a food dish belonging to the missing cat.

Having the photograph with the bright aura, then the vibration of the energy, I can often trace the movement of the cat. (I do need to act as quick as possible, this energy signature can soon be lost; rain is my enemy, it will wash away the trace pattern and leave me with no directional markers.)

Mr. Green had gone missing in the middle of the summer, it was totally out of character, he was a home loving cat with little need to stray.

Because I was called in early I was able to establish he was still alive, his energy was still strong and I was able to retrace his paw steps to a location where the energy just stopped.

The likelihood was he had got into a car, or a van and had been transported to a different area, an area which was unfamiliar. No scent trail, no way back home.

All we had to do was work out the movements of the people who lived closed to the last known location Mr. Green had been.

Like all searches I need a little luck, which on this occasion I had.

A couple had been having a brand new conservatory built on their house, very near to the location where I felt Mr. Green had vanished from. The company had its headquarters four miles away, where it kept all of the work vans overnight.

That was the area we had to look. So Racheal and Linda put up posters in that location and the next day a member of the public rang Linda to say that she had seen Mr. Green that same day.

Two hours later Mr. Green was back home, reunited with the family and the very grateful owners.

He had been taken for a ride, four miles away! All the work, the searching had been worthwhile.

Finding a lost cat is time consuming, it is also very emotional, and people love their pets. But once the cat has been returned the owners very seldom stay in touch. Although Linda did on this occasion. Mr. Green is still alive and well to this day as far as I know, none the worse for his time away.

Cheech

Not every story has a happy ending. This is the story of 'Cheech' the African Grey Parrot who flew out of the kitchen door in his bid for freedom one day and in the process lead myself and Alison on a merry dance across the local country side.

Sky High

The routine is familiar, the phone will go and a voice on the other end will sound distressed, anxious. A story will then emerge of a missing pet, on this occasion it was 'Cheech', the Grey Parrot.

The owner had forgotten that the kitchen door was open when she went to clean out his cage, as soon as the wire door lifted 'Cheech' was gone, out of the kitchen door, settling on a high conifer tree in a neighbour's garden.

New found freedom established he had flown away in a direction unknown. The owner was heartbroken.

The photograph was positive, Cheech still had a strong energy signature. He was alive. So all I had to do was search the local area and with Alison's help we set out on foot to see if we could spot the grey bird.

Spotting a bird is hard enough, catching a bird is just about impossible. I was not about to climb trees!

You just know when you reach the limits of your own capabilities.

Alison was not about to give up on Cheech. Alison phoned the local newspaper who agreed to run a story on this psychic who was looking for an African Parrot.

"If anyone saw him could they please contact Alison?"

We always went the extra mile to help, and this again would happen with Cheech.

Alison had volunteered to go and visit anyone who reported a sighting. I had work to do, and if I was honest I could not see how we could ever find this bird, and even if we did, how would we ever catch it?

Alison was made of sterner stuff, and never gave up hope of receiving that one phone call that would lead her to the location, her mind was fixed; that bird was not getting away.

This is how Alison tells the rest of the story in her own words:

'The lady on the end of the phone was sure, the bird in the paper was in her garden. It was highly likely, her house was only two miles due south as the parrot flies from where 'Cheech' lived.

I had to go over, there was a chance that I could catch the parrot. It had been away now for three days, the chances were that the bird had not eaten, or rested much during those days. It was bound to be tired.

I put the address into the satnav and drove the five miles to the street and number.

The house was over grown, the front garden looked more like Steptoe's yard than a residential house. The front door faded from red to pink, paint peeling off, blistered with years of neglect.

I lifted the pitted metal knocker, the sound echoed round the hall, as it would if the house had been empty. Footsteps, then the clink of the door chain as the door opened and in the back lit light an old lady with an apron tied around her layers of overhanging fat, cigarette in mouth, unwashed face.

"You better come in." "That bird is still in the hedge, just like I told you."

As I walked into the living room, the smell just hit me, cats everywhere, in the corner next to an old man in a dirty white sleeveless vest, dirty greasy hair, stubble and a large beer belly was a cardboard box with a blanket, stuffed in, a female cat guarding a litter of new born kittens, all eager to feed.

In the mouth of the female cat, 'Cheech', as stiff as a board, and very obviously dead. The cat was just about to feed the poor grey African parrot to her kittens.

If I had been ten minutes earlier 'Cheech' would have still been alive.

The old lady took a look at me, then her cat and prized the dead bird from her jaws. The cat jumped and growled, but let go. She thrust the now dead bird into my hand, "You better take this back to the owner".

I didn't want the bird in my hand, so I asked her if she had a box I could put 'Cheech' in so I could transport the luckless bird back to the lady.

"I only have this" She thrust a red Coca cola six pack, flimsy cardboard torn box at me. The bird went inside, and I did my best to fold the lid shut. I could still see the dead bird, eyeing me up from the side!

I thanked the lady and left, fast.

Intentions

Now my intentions were good. Yes the bird was dead, but as long as I took the bird back to the lady I thought she would be grateful, after all I had gone to so much trouble to find 'Cheech', and it was not my fault the cat had got him before I had a chance to save him.

Here I was driving, 'Cheech' in the red Cola box next to me on the passenger seat, jumping up in the air every time I went over a speed bump, I thought he was going to end up on the floor, one hand on the steering wheel, the other on the lid of the box trying to hold the bird in.

Slowing down to negotiate another speed bump, I realised the lady in the car across the road was the same lady who owned Cheech. She had heard her pet had been found and was driving across to the house I had just come from. I pulled over and waved, I could see she was surprised to see me.

I started "I have Cheech, I'm so sorry", the words hardly having time to leave my mouth. The lady snatched the box, peered inside and let out an almighty scream, "Cheeeeeeeech!" and burst into tears. Got in to her car and drove off. Not even a word of thanks. I was dumfounded. I could not believe her reaction, nor what I had just been through.

It took me a while to get over the events of that week. I had only wanted to help, but nothing as strange as folk. Needless to say 'Cheech' was the last bird I ever looked for.'

Still Searching

I still get requests from people to find missing objects, pets and people. I will always help whenever I can. I have learnt you can be placed in a difficult position. Not every missing call has a happy ending.

Desire

In my 'day to day' life I talk with many people. I have noticed a common theme running through our discussions. 'Desire'.

Now, the thing is it's now wrong to want. In fact, it can be very healthy to look around and see what can be achieved if you are prepared to put your all into something.

'Wanting now' is wrong. The people I have been helping struggle with the need to have as soon as they desire. Believing that if they do not have what they want in an instant, they will go without forever.

This is wrong thinking. We can have anything. If we are prepared to work, plan and appreciate. Appreciation is everything

Making headlines.

Talking Auras.

Some of my books.

Working on Stage.

The Paranormal Uncut
radio show with Alison.

Massive orb before a
stage show.

Working at the BBC.

Television.

Very proud to be
considered a friend to the
Queen of Malaysia.

The best wife a man
could wish for.
Dominic and
Alison on their
wedding day.

My father.

My Childhood
Room 2016.

Working at King's
College
Cambridge 2016.

My old school –
Cambridgeshire.

Energy healing
this beautiful horse
– 'Footsteps in the
Sand'.

A different kind of spirit in Australia.

Australia Zoo.

Perth, Australia.

On tour in
Brisbane,
Australia.

Alison in Brisbane,
Australia.

Angel Art.

Angel Art.

Alison and her
late mother
Diana. Two of
the best.

Alison
dowsing in
the haunted
Scole Hotel,
Suffolk

The haunted mill in
north Norfolk.

Relaxing with nature.

Alison's mother
Diana.

Ghost in Berlin
at the Jewish
Memorial.

Working at Aura
Nightclub, Mayfair,
London.

My favourite work,
healing horses.

Alison and Dominic

Platform Medium.

Ghost House
Orb

Playing Cricket
in Sri Lanka

Aura Reading Live on
Stage

CHAPTER NINE

Seeing Auras

In this next chapter I will detail the method used to see 'Auras'. Then I will go on to explain the meanings of each different colour.

We all have an aura, and since I was young I have seen the different colours which vibrate from the energy we radiate, the voice vibration when we speak.

This insight into my world of colour can help you learn to see auras for yourself.

Take another Look.

How much do we really see?

We go from one moment to the next without taking too much notice of our surroundings.

A simple test is to recall what people around us were wearing.

Can you remember what colours your boss was dressed in?

Or the colour of your partners clothes? We are so consumed by how we are feeling, failing to notice others.

It's true.

How many woman are pre-occupied by make up or hair styles?

We are all at it.

It seems nobody notices anyone else; we are all too busy looking at ourselves.

So how can we change this in order to notice what is right in front of us, the colours everybody gives out?

I have never come across anyone other than myself who can see auras.

This doesn't mean no one can, I just haven't met them yet.

Like anything in life we can learn to pick up on the signs, become aware of how to interpret the energy and start to pick up the colours coming from every single object. It's knowing where to start. So much to learn but wanting to know everything.

We want to see auras instantly.

Our knowledge of the aura is very limited.

We know it's a part of who we are.

Energy

We know energy surrounds our bodies.
Most of us know it comprises of different shades of colour.
These colours indicate how we feel.
But how do we start to see first our own aura then the aura of others?
Seeing is believing.
You need to see your own aura so you can trust the idea that if you work hard it will be worth it.
Like anything, we have a limited attention span, so don't try too hard at first.

Practice

Short bursts of practice is far better than continuously long periods of staring ahead. So when you start limit yourself to ten to fifteen minutes. This can be built up over a few weeks, but I know once you start seeing auras you will want to see even more.

To start with you will need a few simple things –

A blackboard (or dark background) which will help you see the outline. When you become more focused you won't need a dark background.

Start with a potted plant.

Plants

Plants have amazing auras and unlike people don't move, complain or need the toilet!
You will also need some cut flowers.
This will help you see how the aura changes as the flowers die.
This might sound cruel, but believe me once you start seeing auras you will think it's what you want to see. A changing aura will show you you're seeing something different every day and know it's not your imagination.
Plant auras are very delicate, very soft colours, so you need to find yourself a table with no direct light, away from windows without curtains.
Too much light around you will make it far harder to see outlines.
You can't see a torch in daylight.
A dimly lit room is best to start with.
Put the blackboard or dark background behind the plant.

Then close your eyes for about a minute, (use this time to focus your mind on what you're about to do.)
Then open both eyes and look at one part of the plant.
A flower or a leaf is the best place to start with.
After a few moments you will start to see a pale outline.
It's normally green or white when you first see it.
Once you have the outline of the area you're looking at take your focus out slightly to include more of the plant until you can see the mist all around your plant.
As your eyes get more and more used to seeing the mist you will start to pick up on colours and different depths of colour.
Each plant has a different feel to it but the focus is the same.
Remember, a dimly lit room is the best way to get your eyes adjusted.

Flowers

Now try the cut flowers.

Place the vase in front of your dark background and go through the same procedure.
Set everything up then close your eyes, focus for about a minute, then look directly at one flower before moving your gaze out to whole vase.
This time you may possibly see a change in the colours of the aura.
If the flowers are fresh, you will see the outline in pale light colours.
Whites, greens, yellows are common colours that you will pick up on.
If the flowers are a few days old you will start to see the colours fade, the whites will start becoming grey, then darker grey, then light black before turning a deep black.
It's good for you to see the change over a few days. Watching a flower die isn't something we do every day, it can only be experienced when you start to open up to the colour fields around the object.
It will give you a different way of looking at cut flowers.
So now you have had your first glimpse of a living aura.
It's amazing.
You will never look at the world in the same way again.
But after a while you will start to look around your local area.
You will see plants in a totally different way.
Even grass becomes interesting.

Emerald Green

The emerald green aura is unlike any other shade of green I have ever seen.
Remember the colours you are seeing are created by the energy of the plant
vibrating at different pitches, thus creating colours.
Every living object has its own vibrational pitch.
This includes minerals, water and the gases we breathe.
Now you are seeing plant auras the next step is to start looking at bigger
plants and animals, before we move on to people.
Trees and animals are a major part of the world we live in.
From the birds in the garden to the pets we live with.
For this next part having a pet of your own will help.
But it's not essential.
But you will have to seek out a tree, and animals in your local area.
I have found parks fantastic places to study auras.
All forms and levels of life congregate there.
Sunset is the best time to start attuning your eyes.
At the beginning finding out where to look will help, dimly lit areas allow
you to find the outline of the aura. Starting with smaller trees focus your
eyes in the same way as you did with the pot plant and flowers.
Standing far enough away to see the whole tree (remember you're starting
small, a five to six foot tree is ideal.)
Look at one area first then gradually allow your eyes to open up to see the
whole tree.
This might mean you walking backwards, so before you start just make
sure your backwards path is clear, so you can move back a few steps
if necessary.
This might take a few goes.
The dark sky in the background will help. Later when you have found your
focusing point you won't need the dark sky back drop.
The rewards are truly wonderful.
Trees have some amazing colours, each tree has a different feel and as you
progress to larger older trees you will start seeing the colours getting
deeper and deeper.
You will notice so much more.

Trees

Trees are full of life.

Squirrels running up then down, insects that buzz around the branches, birds with bright coloured voices. All emit a light colour signature.

Picking up on the kaleidoscope of colours opens up another world.

Please don't give up if nothing is happening for you.

Like meditating, some can with ease, some take a little while to get the hang of focusing.

But most achieve.

You're not trying to find something, it's already there, and it's just a case of teaching yourself something new.

Mastering auras will help you in so many different ways,

You have now come a long way.

From knowing a little about auras, to seeing auras around plants, you know the aura is a unique colour signature surrounding every single object we see.

By choosing to look at a deeper level it's now time to move onto people with a little help from our pets.

What do we want to get from our new found skill?

Do we want just to marvel at the wonders of the universe, seeing colours where we only used to see dull familiar objects?

I doubt this would be enough.

What we want is to be able to work out what others may be thinking or who is compatible to us.

Auras in Action

What does this man's aura tell me about him?

Can I trust him?

The questions are never ending.

But one step at a time.

Just because you can play chop sticks on the piano doesn't mean you are about to play Mozart.

Taking one step forward is all about learning one piece at a time.

Let's first try our skills on an animal.

Have a good look at your pet whilst they are sleeping.

(If you don't have a pet borrow one!)

The hardest thing we do is focus. Animals move around and so does the energy field around them.

If we can get them to stay in one place long enough we can learn where to focus.

About ten centimetres above the back or head is the best place to start.

A dark blanket or background will help you, the outline of an animal is very similar to that of a person.

Three Levels

The aura has three different levels.

The outer aura is what you will see first.

Light orange is the first colour, followed by pale yellow, and light grey, then white turning to very pale pink the closer to the animal you look.

Animals have very simple auras which reach out about ten centimetres, if happy and content. It's good to see what a basic healthy aura looks like. (Very few humans have a basic healthy aura.)

Knowing this makes it easier to interpret human auras later on.

Your pet's aura will change from time to time, when hungry, or tired, excited or upset. All of these basic emotions exist in our animals.

Keep watching them during their daily routine, you will soon pick up on the colour changes.

Before too long you won't even be thinking about looking, you will automatically react to what you are seeing.

This should give you a brand new understanding of your pet.

You now have the basic knowledge you need to start looking at human auras.

This is where we start having to work a little more.

People don't stand still. They talk, often using language to disguise how they are feeling.

It takes on a different feel when you are hearing one thing yet seeing another in their aura.

We have to learn to trust what we are seeing, not hearing.

Peoples' auras are complicated.

When we first start reading human auras we need all the help we can get.

The outer aura is very much the same in all people. An orange shell. So if we first look for the orange this will guide us towards the depth.

The same things apply to humans as apply to plants, trees and animals.

The more alive we are the brighter the colours.

When you first look at a person's aura try to start with a younger person.

These auras are very often similar to that of our pets.

Its only as we get older the aura becomes full of attachments, or holes, children may have an untainted view on life until about seven years old.

The orange outer aura is light pastel and the energy inside light grey or white with touches of blues and yellows with a very pale pink inner aura.

Children

Of course children vary.
But once you have the ability to see the aura your knowledge of how to read the colours will follow.
The same method applies.
Focus your thoughts.
Allow your eyes to adjust, focus on one small part of the person.
An arm or a hand. Then open up your sight to the whole of the person.
Because we are all humans there are two exercises we can practice on ourselves.
The first exercise is to feel the depth of aura.
Take your left hand and hold it flat out in front of you, palm up.
Take your right hand and hold it over your left hand, palm down.
Now move your right hand slowly away in an upwards direction.
What you will feel is the heat of your aura coming from your left hand.
The heat will start off hot and get cooler as the right hand moves further away.
When the heat stops that's the outer part of your aura.
Try this a few times it will get you used to feeling the energy and the depth your aura has around your hands.
Now hold your right hand out in front of you. Close your eyes and focus then open both eyes and fix your gaze on the tip of your middle finger.
Again it helps when you first start to use a black background.
You should see a white glow around the tip of your finger.
The more you practice this the sooner you will start to see the white light splitting into colours, like looking at light passing through a prism.

Building a Picture

By now everything you have learned will be coming together, you are now ready to take your skills into the world you inhabit.
Next it's time to prepare you for what you may see in others and how to interpret what the different colours mean.

Meaningful Colours

The whole world is full of colour.

Who doesn't like watching the sun rise or set?

The beautiful colours blend into one another creating new even more wondrous colours.

The food we eat is only appealing because of the colours we see before we eat.

Colours mean so much to all of us.

The colours of the aura are even more remarkable.

Once your eyes and mind are tuned into picking up the colours of the aura you will never watch another sun rise in the same way. Watching people, animals, even plants will be just as amazing.

But what do the colours of the aura mean?

How can we interpret the mixtures of the cotton candy swirls which flow from the body?

In this chapter I will attempt to explain the meanings of the different colours, then the combinations of colours you might see. Understanding the meanings will help you work out what you are looking at and how this knowledge will help you in your daily life, enabling you to make good decision when interacting socially and personally.

COLOURS – A brief description

Dark Blue

Is often seen in the middle aura. It's all about communication, people who have dark blue are very strong in their use of language and make good debaters

These people are stubborn, believing their views are the right ones.

Blue

Very person based. Would love to share views, help others.

Open to new ideas and to change. People who have blue middle auras will work as writers or teachers and have a very clear view of right and wrong, very rarely do they step out of line preferring to take the safe secure route through life.

Make good partners, but can be dull.

Light Blue

A light blue aura is all about living in a fantasy world.
These people will have their heads in the clouds, day dreamers. Non-confrontational, very laid back approach to any problems.
Make good friends but not that ambitious.

Dark Red

Impulsive. Unpredictable.
Can easily become addicted to frills, would live for the moment.
Would take risks without thought.
Can have anger issues from past mistakes.
Dark red auras can be very attractive people, it's easy to see why others would want to be around these people, but dangerous, only loyal to themselves.

Red

Can be hard to understand, would start off relationships fast, not wanting partners to see too far into them.
Passionate to extreme.
Past issues will play a part in emotional decisions.
Can be loners in life, not trusting other people's judgement.
Would have low self-esteem, need reassurance on a regular basis.
Most red people have issues with others, but keep them well below the surface until they feel safe.

Light Red

Light red auras are very rare, these people have no passion about life.
Will stay alone often choosing very few friends.
People who don't make decisions, tend to stay where they feel safe. Not easy to get on with.
Can lack social skills, I believe this is why you don't come across light red auras.

Dark Pink

Dark pink auras are mixtures of emotions.
People who have not worked out their own sexuality or are very confused over emotions.
Have an outward going personality, can be very loud and in your face type, which when you first meet them can be over whelming.
You would never be bored, but you might never feel that safe, life would be full of ups and downs.

Pink

Good balance, would love life, outgoing, social.
Have a Strong approach to achieving.
Never be fooled by a pink aura, even though the person would come across as less than knowledgeable these people have always done their homework.
They make great partners in life and business, never asking anyone to do something they wouldn't themselves.
Honest, straight forward with an edge. Hard to fall out with unless you're unreasonable.

Light Pink

No so driven, but personality would be good.
Would prefer to be lead. Loyal, kind and gentle. Life would be fun, childlike at times.
Sense of humour and very few confrontational moments.

Dark Green

When you look at a person who drinks a lot of caffeine you see a green aura, it also comes from alcohol, cigarettes, artificial colourings, sugar and even too much fat in the diet.
People with dark green auras eat too much of the quick fix foods and will be drawn to stimulants, tending to have gaps in their outer aura.

Green

Not as Strong as above but with green it's the wrong balance in the diet.
Too much tea coffee or coke, not enough exercise.
People who spend their day sitting down have green inner auras.

Light Green

I don't see many adults who have light green, it's mainly children, animals and plants.
I believe the air we breathe is light green.
When we have very little else polluting our bodies this colour will show up.
Very lime green in an aura only shows up when I see people who live away from civilisation.

Orange

The outer aura.
What you are looking for is a strong outer aura.
Bright orange with a glow is the sign of a fit and healthy person.
It's also one of the easiest colours to pick up on because everyone has an orange outer aura.

Yellow

Very open, easy to be around.
People who have a yellow inner aura are at peace with themselves.
They have found who they are and willing to share knowledge with others.

Dark Yellow

Knowledge seekers.
Dark yellow or gold is about finding truths.
Often these people will like to travel, have an interest in how others live.
Teachers, spiritual healers and peace makers.
Seeing yellow in the inner and outer aura is very often a person who has grown enough not to judge others.
The only down side is these people can attract more dominate reds and blue aura people to them.

Light Yellow

Is often very spiritual. Make fantastic healers.
The yellow energy at this level is very pure, almost untainted, there will be an innocence about how they view life.
Can be very idealistic and might not live in the real world.
But would be a joy to live with as life would be very simple.

They would have few possessions. Wouldn't value money.

Purple

Beware of purple auras.
These people would like to think of themselves as being somebody they are not.
They don't have the ability to find their own way and will attach to other people's ideas or teachings.
Repeating knowledge rather than instigating what they might think.
Often loners who don't fit in socially.
Can be very controlling of others, hiding behind helping.
On the plus side if you see a strong purple aura try to remember not to get too close.

Violet

The same as above with a little less intent.
Violet people tend to keep themselves to themselves.
Will not have personal opinions but adopt opinions of others.
Easily lead, but will often form friends with stronger dark blues.
Not that good in social situations.
Frustrated communicators.

Dark Brown

Is the nearest you will see to black in an aura.
Changeable to extreme, moody, difficult, often intent of worrying about what they can't achieve.
Can get involved with addiction in order to find something that excites or helps them forget.
Will make the same mistakes over and over again.
Beware of Dark Brown at work, they tend to be bullies.

Brown

Not good at communicating.
Will eat to feel better.
People who are unhappy and then eat to change their moods will be brown.
The emotional difficulties will show in the weight of the person.

Light Brown

On the edge of wanting to be different.
Light brown can be highlighted with light yellow which indicates the person could go either way depending on the people they surround themselves with.
Lots of promise to be realised or could go the other direction and become lacking in responsibility.

Dark Grey

Lacking sleep.
This person's energy has been drained by a long emotional battle with people close to them.
Can show unwell in areas of the body.
When Grey replaces more vibrant colours it mean the energy isn't being replaced.

Light Grey

Is temporary, just shows that the person is tired at that moment.
Could be they haven't eaten for a few hours. If you see light grey with holes in the outer orange aura it means the person is at the beginning of a virus or has had a long period of hard work or study.

White

The pureness of aura energy, untainted.
You will see clear energy around people's inner aura, but its normally only reserved for very young babies.
Once life starts to become more involved the white aura will start to give out pale blues and light pinks.
What we must always remember is that the aura is made up from three parts (outer, middle, and inner) it is very rare just to see one colour.
But what you do get are dominant colours.
These are the colours you are looking for.
The over lapping colours can sometimes give you a false impression, so look out for the middle aura, this is where you will get the best indication of the persons personality.

The inner aura closest to the skin is light white or grey, inside these areas you will see what the person has been eating or even any injures the person might be surfing from.

Sports men and women are good to look at, as their inner aura can show signs of wear in the legs and shoulders.

The outer aura is orange but can be seen with the blues, reds and greens effecting the shade of the orange. If the outer aura is wearing thin or has gaps in then this is an indication the person isn't looking after themselves, either pushing too hard or not allowing enough time for recovery, or taking an artificial aid like pain killers or caffeine.

Different colours show this very clearly.

AURA PHOTOGRAPHIC PROFILING (APP)

If you have read the previous chapter on 'finding missing objects' I refer to 'photographic profiling'. Here I explain a little more about reading photographs.

Photographic Auras.

Being able to read an aura is something which we cal all do with practice and patience.

The harder we work the easier it becomes.

If we are not people watchers before we start learning about auras we will soon become so.

I will spend many hours watching people. Looking at their auras, watching their actions. Often the colours will show intent. Most of what we do we never think about.

When was the last time you thought about how you walk or breath?

Body language can tell us much about how people are, even the Chinese art of face reading which goes back hundreds of years can give us clues to what lays beneath.

But auras don't lie. Cannot be manipulated.

The energy we give out of our bodies is showing the world everything we are.

People watching is a good way of learning the meanings of the colours.

But there is another way.

Every time a photograph is taken it captures the energy which is the aura.

A freeze frame of a moment in time.

A photograph will show you how the person was at the exact moment in time the photograph was taken.

Learning how to read the colours captured in the frame can be a valuable asset in understanding how that person was feeling and even thinking when that photograph was taken.

So how do we start to understand photographs?

Aura reading is about focus. The more we look the more we see.

Photographs are no different.

To start with I would recommend a large colour photograph of just one person A4 is a good size. (You will move on to more complicated photos in time but first let's get your eyes and mind tuned into the process.)

First choose a darkened room, no natural direct light, so draw the curtains.

Not pitch black just enough light to see the objects in the room with you.

Close your eyes for about thirty seconds. This will help you eliminate the light from your eyes before you look at your photograph.

Privilege

Seeing auras is a privilege, a remarkable understanding which will enhance your life, guide you and help you. Well worth changing how you see and think.

DIANA – 1931 – 2017

December 2017 was a very sad time for Dominic and myself as my mother, Diana passed away at the age of 86 years.

Diana had an open mind to spirituality, although it did unnerve her a little bit.

Towards the end of her life she did mention seeing 'smiling faces' in her bedroom, and children running along the corridor, seeming comfortable sharing this with me. However Diana was very private, kept a lot of her thoughts to herself and we never discussed the 'after life'.

My mother's funeral was in January 2018, after which we experienced a lot of activity in our home. At first the odd log fell from the fireplace and candles vigorously flickered, nothing that untoward, but the start of some strange happenings.

Diana, prior to her passing had given me her bunch of house keys which I kept in my handbag. For security reasons we had decided to change the locks on her front and back doors, so the old bunch of keys became 'redundant' so to speak, so we threw them in the dustbin.

A few weeks passed and Dominic and I then went to the cemetery to collect my mother's ashes. I had dreaded doing this and somehow felt rather nervous that morning.

We sat in a very peaceful room, waiting for the lady to bring the ashes to us, sitting in silence. On my lap I had my handbag and kept jiggling my car keys, wanting to get out as quickly as possible. As I 'twiddled' my car key for the umpteenth time I couldn't believe what I was seeing, attached to the key ring – Diana's back door key!

I knew immediately by the shape and discolouration it was definitely her old key. I was astonished. How on Earth could this happen? I had 'binned' the whole bunch a few weeks earlier! This was incredible; and I had seen the dustbin lorry collect, then drive away. For myself it was mind blowing, as I hadn't experienced anything like this before. I kept trying to think of any logical explanation, but couldn't. I came to the conclusion it was my mother, Diana wanting me to keep her backdoor key she had used for 40 years and wasn't happy I had put it in the bin. She had 'teleported' her key onto my key ring on the day we were collecting her ashes to get our attention. She certainly did that, and I've kept if there ever since.

I know we all connect to the universe through 'thought'; and our thoughts travel for all of us to 'tap into' if we are wanting to – well, just after the 'key' episode I wanted other 'signs or signals' from Diana to make her presence known to me. I often talk to her in my head as if she was present in the room, but I suppose I needed something to happen when I asked for it.

We were watching a DVD (The History of Norwich), which my mother would most certainly have enjoyed, when suddenly the DVD player switched off. At first I wondered if there had been a power cut, and start pressing buttons to turn it back on again. I said in my head 'if this is you mum, can you turn it on again?' Within seconds the DVD continued as normal. I repeated this a few times in my head, and each time the DVD went on, then off whenever I asked. This certainly wasn't a co-incidence.

We had a 'quiet' period for a while then the spirit activity started up again.

I had purchased several beauty products from Boots the Chemist, along with a jumper, and put them all in the same plastic bag, placing it in the back of the car. On reaching home only the jumper was in the bag, no beauty products! I had the receipt and rang the chemist to see if maybe I had left them on the counter – but no I hadn't. Now the Toyota car I own used to belong to Diana and it's always been clean and tidy, with no rubbish on the floor or seats; in lovely condition. So my last look for the 'missing' beauty products would be in the car; and I would see straight away if they were there.

Diana only put food shopping on the back seat, and rarely did anyone sit in the back. As I peered in the back a large pink spotted umbrella was laying in full view on the seat, which wasn't there that morning! You may think that's not unusual, but it wasn't my umbrella, nor being 'pink spotted' would belong to Dominic. I picked it up, looked at the 'designer make' and knew it was a family member's umbrella. This relative had a lot of items with the same design on. It certainly didn't make sense how the umbrella came to be in the car, as the family member hadn't ever been in the car with me.

I mulled things over, but decided at that time not to do anything and put a raincheck on it (excuse the pun!)

After discussing this with Dominic he told me he found two golf balls in the same spot where the umbrella was a week earlier – but I doubt Diana had been playing a round of golf! We put it down to Diana again 'teleporting' items and being active in the car. I never found my beauty products; maybe they ended up in someone else's car – who knows!

The following day I got in the car and drove to the supermarket. I put the groceries in the boot and got back in the car, then started the engine. Suddenly I got the fright of my life as a 'voice'; speaks to me from the glovebox. It takes me a few seconds to recover and realise it's the SAT NAV. Now this was weird as it was unplugged and turned off. It was one of the old type which only works if plugged into the cigarette lighter, so no way was it charged up. It was unbelievable. After the initial shock I continued home with the SAT NAV shouting directions from the glove box. I got home, parked up and only then did I open the glove box to see it switched on and active. I knew it was my mother Diana, again showing me her presence; and I know she wants me to recognise that too.

We often get the odd item moved to get our attention, or things going missing; and I don't think either of us has seen the end of it; it's always expecting the unexpected.

In December 2018 it will be the first anniversary of Diana's passing; although we know you are still with us, and you are only a 'thought away'.

Alison Zenden

Fish trap

Circumstances can lead us into many difficulties. We may not always realise it at the time, but what we are going through can lead to what we think is a 'way out' when in reality it is a dead end.
We must be aware of 'fish trap' relationships. The fish trap has a narrow entrance which the fish can swim easily into, the bait is enticing, a meal which hasn't had to be worked for. Then the catch, the small entrance does not allow for the fish to escape.
I have come across many relationships which start in this way. The promise of something that only leads to giving over your own self will.
All relationships have to be an exchange. It is vital you get to know the person, their circumstances, their family and friends. Their visions, their dreams. Red flags should be taken notice of. No friends, bad previous relationships, dysfunctional parents. Are only a few flags you should be aware of.
Know that you can find your way out, but it takes a strong minded individual with lots of determination.

CHAPTER TEN

Families

I see humour in most areas of life. By slowing myself down I notice so much more. My personal thoughts on humour I believe are bringing people together and lifting the atmosphere in a room to a different level.

There is however a balance to be found. Dying is a serious business, and people can get upset if the passing of a relative is treated in a somewhat flippant manner. A stage medium treads a narrow plank. Not enough humour and the audience can lose attention and start chatting amongst themselves. Too much humour and you are touching on the ground of the standup comedian. A fine balance between respectful and funny.

Next time you sit in an audience try to remember the funny times you spent with your family. Every single person can remember laughing uncontrollably at funny family moments which were just spontaneous.

I love these funny stories when they come through. I know my family has a few which my late father would enjoy reeling out every time the extended family got together.

I will not share all the stories detail by detail, just this one.

It was me at the age of four whilst on a family outing to see the lions in one of those drive through safari parks, sat innocently on the ground eating the picnic lunch which had been packed up carefully by parents and grandparents. I pointed and shouted, "There's another lion!" It was a large Golden Labrador dog, which just happened to look like a lion to a four year old child. But I did wonder why the adults turned white and over reacted, gathering the rug and food up rather fast!

My father would say his mother, my grandmother never forgot this and would often point to Labradors in the street, exclaiming; 'there's another Lion'. It would make her laugh.

This is the kind of family story which lightens the mood and brings people together. I think we have all sat through mediumship demonstrations which have been extremely dull, boring and unforgettable.

The skill of the medium is to keep the audience engaged, whether you like it or not you have chosen to entertain. If you feel uncomfortable with this then do not do stage work. Every medium affects every other medium. What I say or do impacts on all other working mediums. I accept this.

My dream is that all spiritualists come together, work for the same course, providing evidence beyond doubt of the existence of 'life after life'. No ego, no hiding behind spiritualism as a personal identity. Just good honest proof.

The Hairdressers

Talking about good honest proof, a few years back I would work on a Tuesday morning from a small room above a hairdressers. The people who ran the shop were lovely warm folk. Husband and wife, hardworking people who had built their business over many years.

The shop itself was old, parts of it went back to the fifteenth century. The upstairs had a lovely, friendly energy, and was the ideal place to work from as a medium.

The people who came into the shop for their cut and blow dry would book me for private readings and I would share the small fee with the owners. As I have said before, working as a medium is not a way of becoming a millionaire. It is a way of life you choose because of the rewards you get from watching people react with joy when a loved one comes through.

The salon provided me with a steady stream of clients. The tiny room, just big enough to fit two chairs a small table and my tape recorder. I would always tape every sitting, people could not always remember the information brought through, and I certainly would not remember. As soon as the words have left my mouth I am ready for the next line.

Ghost - House had taught me about working hard, I would start work at about four in the afternoon, take the groups around the house, then when all that had finished I would take myself off into a little room and perform private one to one readings until the next morning. I would work solidly from midnight to eight the next morning, the line outside my room waiting for their turn would stretch ten or so deep, no break just one person after another until breakfast.

That was working.

Doing a couple of readings on a Tuesday morning was easy.

Evidence

Every sitting was different. Each person expectant.

I have little personal recollection of the details of the readings. People would come and go, each would be pleased with the outcome of their visit. I would hear back from the owners of how impressed they had been, how they had not experienced so much detail before. All very nice. Praise is something I find difficult.

One funny story which stuck in my memory was that of a middle aged lady. The tiny room and small chair had struggled to cope with fitting her into the room. But with a squeeze and a more intimate closeness than normal I had navigated my way through a number of her late relative's messages. The outstanding evidence being brought forward by her father. The sitting had gone well and I expected the lady to be pleased with what she had just heard. But you know when you get the feeling that someone did not want to leave? Well I got this with her. She wanted more?

I could hardly move, the small table had been pushed up against my knees, my chair as far back as it could go, this lady was wedged in between the back of the door and the table, which was now hovering in midair, caught between the two of us. I was not going anywhere until this lady stood up and opened the door!

One last go, deep breath, "I think we have made some fabulous connections" I began, then in a moment of madness went on to list the various people who had made an appearance, ending with, "the only person who has not come through was your mother". I had no sign of anyone who was her mother. She looked at me and started laughing. "I hope not, she was very much alive when I left her downstairs get her wash and set!"

The reason this woman had not wanted to leave was because she knew her mother was going to be another ten minutes under the hairdryer! The thought of her mother directly underneath the room where we were sat plugged into a hairdryer just made me laugh. Luckily the woman also found it amusing and in a way added to the credibility of the reading.

Taught me a good lesson, never to assume anything, oh and to make sure the room I was working in was big enough for me to move.

Challenge

Those of you who have met me know how much I like a challenge. Being able to baffle or bemuse those who doubt (or just do not believe in an afterlife) I personally class as a challenge. I have never argued with anyone, no point. We believe in what we experience, right?

My best weapon is the information given over by spirit. I have found that the best evidence is personal, and the best way to present it is when a person is not expecting. I get the most honest reactions then.

This is a story of meeting a man on holiday and how one piece of information changed how he saw mediums.

Holidays

Going away does not fill me with joy. I dislike airports full stop, the crowds, the waiting and then the tightly packed flights. How do airlines get so many people into one small space? There is nothing nice about sitting next to strangers coughing and children crying.

Then when you have endured all of this you have the scrum at the other end to collect your luggage, and finally the long wait to book into your hotel room, often late at night. You then discover that your hotel room looks out, not over the beach or sea, but the hotel kitchen. Welcome to the world of package holidays!

All of the above had happened to us on this trip to Cyprus.

I am not complaining, being able to travel is a privilege, one which my parents did not have. Travel certainly educates. But I have never subscribed to the view that holidays are stress free zones where you can relax.

Cyprus is a country of superb views, the people are friendly, hotels clean. Only a few hours away by plane. Most of the people we met in the hotel were British, a few Germans and some Dutch, but mainly people like myself, middle class working folk away for a few days sun.

Making friends was easy, conversations flowed over the breakfast buffet, or on the sun beds around the pool.

I have long realised people like to talk about themselves, why wouldn't they? It makes my life easier, all I have to do is nod and listen as 'well-rehearsed often told' stories are trotted out for another outing. I will watch their partner switch off as the lines are too much to cope with for yet another time.

This suits me, I never have liked being asked, "And what do you do?" My mischievous side is always eager to play along with those who doubt or even worse, question. I believe there is little better fun than to find myself in they company of another who is so closed to the prospect of 'life after life' that one piece of information can blow their world of cynicism wide apart.

Place yourself at a hotel breakfast table, a group of newly acquainted friends enjoying the relaxed atmosphere of a warm Cypriot morning. There sat around the table, myself and Alison, an older couple in their early seventies, hypochondriac woman, and her super agreeable second husband.

Young couple, 'up and at them' school teachers, lovely people who were great company, but knew everything. I did not need my computer I just asked them and the answer would be provided.

Inevitably the conversation focused on what I did. I am always happy to explain, and discuss the merits of being a medium. The moments of joy, the sadness of the needy. I will never defend or justify. But very happy to talk about my personal beliefs if asked.

It goes without saying that most hold strong opinions, for or against.

This man, a teacher, was of the firm belief that mediumship was at best tenuous, at worst a skillful con. I can empathise with his point of view. Extraordinary claims take extraordinary proof. I certainly believe that when working as a medium you should never ask questions, read body language or use Barnham statements. (A Barnham statement is a line of dialog designed to cover all possibilities.) A common example for a medium to use is, "I have John with me, who is John?" If you have John why don't you ask him who he is? Many mediums use disguised questioning to uncover pieces of information then claim to be the barer rather than the receiver.

The only way for a medium to achieve credibility is not to look for confirmation, during a sitting. And not to ask questions. The information should come direct from the medium to the sitter.

For a medium to be able to deliver this in a sitting takes extreme focus and skill. I have to use all of my five senses, inner calm, and an unbroken quietness to hear and relay the images, messages and anything else that is shown. Being a medium is not an easy occupation.

Our conversation was not one of difference, it was one of 'I do not talk about the evidence I bring through', as this would have no relevance to this man personally. But I would promise before we left the hotel at the end of the week to share with him some information from spirit that only he and he alone would know. As I said, I love a challenge and I love to make people question their own understanding. On this occasion I had no idea what I was going to tell him, or whether I was going to be able to tell him anything.

I had to wait and listen and have faith in spirit coming through for him, as well as myself.

Hop and a skip

I am my own worst enemy, I place exacting standards on myself and my work as a medium. Here I was on holiday in Cyprus away from the pressures of daily readings and I had decided I was going to do the impossible, change a person's mind about the validity of mediumship.

Breakfast was served, cold meat and slices of cheese, yoghurt and fresh fruit, piles of pastries, hot black coffee. I could not help thinking, this is the same every single day of every single year, whether I am here or not! How boring for the staff, a clock work operation which never changed. The only difference, the faces of the guests.

Alison and I would sit next to our newly acquired friends, just talking about the various day's activities. When my moment came. Messages will often just appear in my thoughts without warning. I have come to recognise, the process. Alison tells me my eyes start to spin, and I go vacant for a few seconds!

It was clear to me what I had to say to my friend. I had been shown a man on a running track, but his legs were covered by a sack. This man was competing in a sack race, but it was not just any sack race, it was an Olympic sack race!

The man in the sack told me his name and went on to show me he had been an Olympic sack race champion.

Brilliant! Evidence beyond doubt.

Now there are some moments as a medium I live for. This was one of them. The look of total astonishment on this man's face was a picture.

Once he had wiped up the spilled coffee which he spat across the crisp white table cloth, he looked at me and just nodded. Yes he confirmed my Grandfather was an Olympic champion in the sack race. But how would you have known that? Only family knew.

I just grinned, a moment of self-satisfaction. Spirit had come through with some extraordinary proof. The man hoping through my thoughts was his Grandfather.

Beyond Reasonable Doubt

I know after our holiday this couple stayed in touch, the man has become a firm believer. He tells anyone who will listen to his tale of proof.

He now faces the same reaction I have come so used to. The sceptics who believe you must have googled the information, or researched the family background. I will never convince those who are of a mindset not to believe.

My holiday friend however will never forget that morning in Cyprus when he had been given a message; proving beyond doubt mediumship is real, and he had been very wrong.

The Old Rectory

In the early 1970's the old rectory next door to my family home was put up for sale.

It wasn't used as a rectory, but a residents seemed to come and go very frequently.

Rumour had it there were lots of ghostly happenings and was known locally as 'the most haunted house in Hertfordshire.

It was the summer of 1974 when a family of six moved into this ivy clad, three storey rectory. The garden was overgrown hiding concrete stone animals throughout the undergrowth and the rectory peering out from somewhere in-between. It wasn't a warm inviting house, rather eerie and gloomy from the outside.

The garden fence ran along the perimeter of my parent's property and I had many spy holes in the fence to peep through.

The new family were French and four children under six years old.

I used to watch the children play through my spy hole and the eldest daughter often lined up dolls on the hammock singing to them in French.

That summer I was about to experience events that I had only heard rumours about. One evening I was asked to babysit and being next door didn't have far to walk. As I entered the overgrown field as it was known shivers ran down my spine and a feeling of uncertainty came over me. As I knocked on the huge brass handle Anouska the doll collector opened the door and stated she was allowed to stay up and play for a while and go later to bed. The hallway was full of taxidermy displayed on the walls and a stags head on the archway to the lounge above with glass starey eyes followed me in there. A very creepy evening was in store for me. The criss cross design windows were ajar and they were squeaking and rattling. Allowing breeze to enter and sway the old net curtains.

During the evening Anouska talked to me about Emily her friend upstairs and took my hand and took me up the old oak staircase. At the top a black cat was curled up on the landing. Unperturbed as their Old English sheepdog kept barking. I cautiously entered Anouska's room and saw the beautifully decorated dolls which I had seen on the hammock a few days before. I asked if one was Emily to which she shook her blond locks and said Emily lives up there (pointing to an annex) and wakes me up to play. I was just fifteen years old so didn't really understand so thought it was just another doll, as she had too many dolls for one little girl to play with.

Twin boys Phillipe and Louis were asleep down the corridor so I said goodnight to their sister and walked to the dimly lit twin's room. It was then I stopped in my tracks as I felt I was being followed. I heard footsteps behind, quickly looked round but no one was there. The floors boards creaked not helping the fear I was feeling.

I remember seeing the boys fast asleep so I tiptoed out intending to go downstairs and watch TV.

Suddenly the footsteps started again and brushed-nylon curtains swished vigorously on the landing knocking a figurine onto the floor. Anouska awoke as she was a light sleeper and said not to close the landing window as the cat needed to come in and out.

I stood frozen not knowing what to do. I picked up the cracked porcelain figure and placed it on the landing table wondering how to explain this to their mother, when Anouska demanded my attention. She spoke first in French, then again in English.

I somehow managed to usher Anouska (Noushy she was called) back into her room.

Her dolls were now in a circle, sitting upright with teacups and saucers in the middle. Noushy said "Emily likes to play with them when I am asleep." From the corner of my eye the dolls crib gently started rocking. Neither of us were near it and heard laughter coming from the annex above. By now I really didn't want to be in that house, although I couldn't show that to a six year old! The hairs stood up on my arms and there was definitely a presence in this room and the landing. Their black cat was pacing up and down, tail swishing and I knew something 'paranormal' was occurring.

Noushy insisted I shout and say 'Goodnight!' to Emily in the attic before she eventually went to bed. I nervously brought her a glass of water and remember my hand shaking as I put it by the bed.

As I left her room I was back on the landing and a long full length mirror with gold edging faced me as I walked towards the stairs. As I glanced in it a cloudy white mist engulfed the centre of the mirror. As my eyes focused a young girls face appeared and we had 'eye to eye' contact. I remember long straight hair surrounding a rather sad expression looking at me. It probably only lasted seconds; but I was transfixed and my heart was beating fast. It faded slowly then just completely vanished, leaving no trace and no explanation. I felt I was dreaming as I have never experienced anything like this.

Their dog growled, looking up at me and the cat, who was now perched on the table with the broken figurine. She was very aggravated and hissed at me! (That terrified me too, I was a nervous wreck!)

I ran downstairs turning every light on, wanting to pick up the phone and ring my mum when I heard tapping on the front window which stopped me in my tracks. I also distinctly heard a loud 'meowing' sound coming from the front. I pulled back the drapes and saw a silhouette of another cat, looking distressed. It was pacing along the ledge looking bedraggled. As I went to let it in it just vanished completely, disappeared.

No trace whatsoever.

Before I had time to think what I had seen car headlights were coming up the long drive; I was so relieved the parents were home. I decided to keep everything to myself as was internally questioning all that had happened, but knew I would never step in that place ever again.

A few months passed and yes I did still peer through the fence, but had no yearning to go the other side anymore.

I had told a few school friends what I had experienced with mixed opinions as you can imagine.

I did however take another babysitting job and confided in Mrs. Jackson about the ghostly happenings in the rectory a few months earlier.

Mrs. Jackson (Susan, but I never called her by her first name, you didn't in those days) was a local teacher in the village. She told me rumour had it that at the turn of the last century (1900) when it was used at a rectory a huge fire had engulfed part of the house and two members of the family had died.

I was fascinated to hear this and wanted to hear more.

"It's only a rumour" she kept repeating, as if to convince me, seeing the look on my face.

She confirmed too that a few years before a pupil who had attended the local school had lived there a short while and often saw a black cat in and out of the house. There one minute, vanishing the next. Questioning what she saw.

A picture of what I'd experienced, mirrored what Mrs. Jackson was telling me.

I later heard that 'The Rectory' in Hertfordshire was mentioned in a local book incorporating many 'ghostly happenings' in our area which had gone on for hundreds of years and a fire certainly had taken the life of a child and her black cat in the annex!

Immediately I knew Anouska's playmate 'Emily' must have been the ghost child I had seen in the mirror; there can't be any other explanation other than an imaginative child's mind.

A year later the French family did move and go back to France I believe. I never did or was never asked to babysit again.

I heard 'business' was the reason for moving, but I do wonder if that was the real reason or just another family that couldn't cope with the 'presences' which still occupied number 13, The Old Rectory. Yes, 13, unlucky for some!

Alison Zenden.

Ghosts

Before I end this chapter I would like to explain a little more about the different types of ghosts you may encounter.

Reply Ghost

This is also known as 'The Stone Tape' ghost. The most common of all the ghosts we may encounter. This ghost is triggered by the atmospheric conditions. It is not real just a replay of a scene from times gone by. It is believed the energy is trapped inside stone or wood. When the right atmospheric conditions occur, 'thunder and lightning' for example, the 'ghost' or ghostly scene is triggered, just like replaying a video tape of an occurrence long since passed. People have been recorded seeing whole legions of Roman troops, or scenes of accidents being replayed right in front of them. This is the energy of this event being released by the atmosphere.

Poltergeist

Or noisy ghost. This ghost wants you to see or hear it. If you encounter a Poltergeist it does not always mean it is sinister, in fact the opposite could apply. Think of it as wanting to be released from the Earth's dimension and making these wishes known. Any senescent life form, which a Poltergeist is likely to be is capable of thought and self-will. Just because we cannot understand how this could be does not mean we should be fearful of it.

If you come across a Poltergeist seek help from a professional who can release it for you.

Shadow Ghost

This type of ghost is rare but not unheard of. It is the negative energy left behind from the soul when the soul transcends to spirit. It looks like a black cloud of dust, moving by itself. Often found in dark corners of old buildings but has been seen in new homes built on old ground. People report of feeling affected emotionally when encountering a Shadow ghost. The atmosphere in a home becomes very dense and repressive. If you think you have a Shadow ghost use light to open up the corners of dark rooms, Shadow ghosts will not stay in well-lit areas.

Living Ghost

This is one of the strangest ghosts you may encounter, the ghost of a living person! These types of ghosts are not rare, many people have experienced seeing a 'Living ghost' or doppelgänger. They are ghosts that carry messages to prevent situations occurring. Messages of hope or consequence. Living ghosts can also fall into the category of 'replay ghosts'. Seeing yourself walking down a street either younger or older is one very odd experience.

Self-Imposed

Most of what happens to us is self-imposed. You can very easily over-think yourself into situations that simply do not exist. Triggers and previous experiences do play a part in how we may interpret daily life, but I have come to understand using past situations to justify current reactions is wrong. Penny Parks talks about this in her book 'Inner Child'. Yes we are left with scars, yes they do affect our behaviour, but as soon as we realise this it's time to deal with the past. Penny then says, 'Carrying around other people's issues is like wearing dirty clothes. No one in their right mind would wish to wear unwashed hand me downs!

Take it from me, learning to let go is the hardest thing we ever think about as an adult.

CHAPTER ELEVEN

Georgios Kyriacos Panayiotou

A wise man once wrote "find a job that you love and you will never have to work a day in your life."

I can relate to that quote, the only difference is the job found me. I never know what the day has in store for me, but when opportunity comes calling to work on radio or television I count my blessings, and enjoy every moment.

This was one of those moments. I had been invited to work for Sky Television on a show which promoted 'psychics and mediumship'. My job would be to present too. A two hour long show twice a week, straight to camera. I would be one of a team of six mediums who would cohost the programme with a producer and an overall manger.

The content was up to me as long as I got the sponsors name in to my presentation four times an hour.

This was so much fun. I would answer questions, perform readings and talk about the paranormal, the audience loved the format. The only sacrifice was that twice a week I would have to leave home at four am to travel to the television studios in London, then drive home again late at night.

I never felt being a television presenter was work, I loved the job, the freedom the work created to meet new people, and of course those who would invite me to meet and read for them. My phone was always busy, and my e-mail account brimming over with offers of work.
Being on television certainly gets you noticed.

During my year long stay on the programme I got to meet so many lovely people, some of who were well known in their industries.

I love people, I am not one who believes that fame makes a person worth knowing. People are people whether or not they are in the public eye, meeting celebrities was exciting, and on a few occasions very disappointing, but never boring.

George

I have a personal rule, I never speak in public about the people I have read for, whilst they are still alive.

Footballers, sportsmen and women, famous couples, record producers, radio hosts, even kings, queens and princesses, all have invited me at some time to read for them. I have travelled thousands of miles to meet and read for some of the most famous people on the planet. All of which must go untold at this time. I value their privacy and the confidential nature of their lives and my involvement with them.

When a person crosses over, leaving this side of life I am happy to write about my experiences with them, and in this man's honour extremely happy to put the record straight on some of the misconceptions which have been written in the press over recent years about him. The only shame is he's no longer here to share his wonderful talent with the world.

I first met George Kyriacos Panayiotou or more commonly known by his working name as 'George Michael' whilst working on psychic television.

I had no idea how much he enjoyed watching. I had always tried to keep my two hour segments as informative as I could. My hands were tied to a certain extent by the broadcasting authorities regarding what I could and could not say. My main ability lay in my mediumship, I would have to word my readings in such a way so they would not be frowned upon by the media regulators. 'For entertainment purposes only.' was the phrase they would have us repeat. Still I would push the rules as far as I could without overstepping the line. I wanted to work in the media.

George first made contacted with me after watching my discussion on merits of mediumship. I have disliked the way mediumship has been promoted or has a way of drawing to it those who are self or ego based. This is the unsavoury side of the work I love being part of. Spirit is uncomplicated, why complicate?

When I first met George I liked him straight away, no ego or rock star syndrome, just a very approachable down to Earth man. He wanted to chat about the possibilities of life after death. Knowledge over hype. I could relate to his thinking, and was able to talk with him. Float ideas and share insights. Our first meeting in North London lasted a lot longer than I had expected, he never asked me to bring anything other than knowledge on that occasion, no mediumship, no empathy, just conversation and company. Over the next few years we would become friends. Nothing was off limits, but I would never contact George. If he wanted to talk or meet I would arrange it, like any of the other people who seek my advice or help I would always make time. After all, most of us can find ten minutes even in the busiest of schedules.

Common Ground

George and I were from the same generation. We both grew up in the seventies, he had gone to school in Watford, England. I knew the area because I had spent some time working there. His father was Greek, mother English and both had instilled a warm generous nature in him. He really was a lovely, genuine man.

It worked well I believe because I have never been star struck, people are people. George was a friend who I could relate too

When I finally got to sit down with George and work with him as a medium I saw a different side. I can remember he had just returned from touring, he was so drained.

Whether or not the demands on his time, or the endless media requests had created this I do not know. But the emotion of what he had experienced was very close to the surface that late summer afternoon.

We all go through losing people, death after all is a matter of fact. But what had hit George hard was the passing of his mother, Lesley. All the success and all the attention had really hampered his ability to cope with such a massive love and influence passing over.

As a medium I would never touch on the status of George's life, but I knew he would have changed everything just to have his mother back.

She had passed over in 1997 from cancer. She was the one person in the whole wide world who had kept George sane. I am not exaggerating. He coped with her death by throwing himself into work. No time to stop, his life style of emotional avoidance had worked well. But right here, right now he had run out of energy.

That day I must have stayed at 'The Grove' for well over the time I had anticipated. The reading was clear, his mother shared some very private family moments, but how do you reach a person who is lost and alone? It all felt rather surreal.

George was such a funny man, his humour mainly self-derogating was hilarious. I would have tears rolling down my cheeks with laughter, sides aching, with rocking. Nothing was off limits and he managed to poke fun at life and himself in equal amounts.

I knew this was his way of dealing with loss, the deep sense of loneliness. His mother was the centre of his own personal universe.

On one hand I could understand his grief, as my father had passed over after a long terminal illness, empathy is little consolation when you see a friend attempting to cover up the still raw emotions which have never been allowed out, and alarm bells do sound.

Twelve Weeks

I left that day worried about George's mental state. I knew he had been smoking too much, not engaging with people, living a secret reclusive life style, sleeping all day and looking for kicks at night. It was clear he had hit the wall.

I hoped the time we had spent together would help him come to terms with losing a parent.

I did not hear from or see George for another twelve weeks. I knew no news was good news. He would have thrown himself into writing and working. He would never know what was happening next, which was a good thing for him, time was his enemy.

So when I received his phone call I was pleased to hear from him.

He was upbeat and cheerful, he was not one to impose, and the purpose of his call was to invite me over to 'The Grove' for lunch. As I was working in London at the time I was happy to stay overnight and visit him the next day.

This was not work, it was pleasure. I looked upon George as a friend and enjoyed debating with him. Conversations could be about anything, but mainly spiritual, life, the universe and other possibilities. He would ask the questions, I would answer setting out my thoughts, philosophies; George would dissect and pick out the bits he wanted to know more about. I can remember having discussions on the soul, and soul connections and relationships. He did not believe in fate even though his life had been turned upsides down by personal relationships.

George was very interested in my work as a past live regressive therapist. How soul groups worked. We also discussed alien life. George was open to the universe being a place full of other intelligent life.

Not a hint of mediumship! Just two friends talking.

Last Time

This was to be the last time I would visit 'The Grove'. But not the last time I would meet or talk with George.

I had a great amount of regard for him. He would tell me about the work he was doing, the charities which he supported, etc. I knew he did not like his individual charitable work being in the public domain. He was a private man.

He also surprised me by presenting two tickets to his concert. You would have had to live on Mars not to know who he was, but I had never really connected the two different sides. To me he was George. To the adoring fans he was a genius. His music was something else. I had explained to him that I would rarely go to places with large amounts of people. I just could not cope with the amount of noise from their thoughts. It is hard to explain, but part of being a medium, how it works is you can pick up vibrations from peoples thoughts. Everything about spirit contact is the power of thought. We never die because our energy is pure thought. That thought exists whether mortal and living on this planet, or spirit in the realm.

George being George was so kind. He provided me with my own V.I.P. box all to myself. This was the only way I could enjoy his performance and after the show he spent time chatting to my family and friends. Nothing was too much trouble for him.

Dark Days

Life for George was never dull. He was loved by everyone he met. He did struggle, especially with the loss of his mother, and two close friends. George's private life will always remain private. I would never write about the things we would discuss in confidence. He might have left this world on Christmas day 2016 but I still feel him around. His music will live on forever. Some people are too special to live. They burn brightly and fast, life is only a passing state before returning home to be at peace.

I treasure the memories, the time spent, even the sharing of common ground. But like George would say himself, I am just an ordinary man who got lucky! He never did see what others saw, he was too busy trying to make sense out of this mad world.

Courage

Last night I was talking with a couple who had lost a teenage son. The courage they showed was incredible. Due to circumstance they had to relocate and start again.

Confessing it had been tough was only the start of our conversation. Where do you make genuine friends? They both asked. At our age all the nice people have their friends. The only people who want to get to know us are the people who are wrapped up in themselves.

They had a point.

I am sure many of us go through this. Second relationships (or new beginnings) are tough. My answer to them was simple, you have each other. Follow your passions. Enjoy the day, and be thoughtful of those you invite in. Nothing really matters.

CHAPTER TWELVE

Paranormal Questions and Answers

Every single day I get asked questions.

In this chapter I have taken some of the more interesting examples.

Each question is from a different person who wants to understand the paranormal better.

Question:

For the last few weeks I have been experiencing something I am struggling to explain. On my bathroom wall I have a rather large mirror, each morning for the last few years I have used this mirror to shave in. Just recently I have started to notice around my head, shoulders and right hand colours being reflected back around them from the mirror. This might not seem that strange, but the colours change. The first day I noticed pale orange, blue and green. As you can imagine I thought no more of this putting it down to a trick of the light, but the next day the colours had slightly changed with green being the more dominate. Over the next couple of weeks I took more notice and kept a mental note of the different shades which seemed to be actively moving around my upper body. I also must add it is only my bathroom mirror that I see this in. Do you have any idea's what this could be?

Barry. Cornwall

Dominic's Reply:

Have you ever considered the possibility that you are seeing your aura? The presence of an aura has not been proven, although it is thought the body produces energy which is projected outside the body. The first documented study of the aura was achieved in 1911 by Walter J. Kilner. He called his work 'The Human Atmosphere' and this published work became the definitive study on auras until recently when my book 'Aura Life in 4D' was published.

What you have described experiencing is the movement of ever changing colours outside your body. These colours are created by the vibration of the energy your body presents. The orange in your account is your outer aura. The outer aura (orange in appearance) is thought to represent the protective shell of the human aura. The blues and greens are more likely to come from your middle and inner aura.

The one thing which convinced me you were seeing your aura was the fact you saw ever changing colours. Our 'aura' is a reflection of everything we are and is forever changing with our different moods. Even the food we eat effects the colours in our inner auras. The one question still remaining is why do you only see this in your bathroom mirror? This could be as simple as the bathroom has a dim light which allows the colours to be reflected. When I teach people how to see 'auras', I start off with a black background, could it be that your bathroom is naturally dark? It is a lot harder to see the aura in an artificial light. Strip lighting seems to camouflage the effect. My thoughts are that during the summer months you have not had the need to switch on your bathroom light.

Question:

The other day I was out shopping with my friends and decided to stop for coffee. The shop was very atmospheric, old wooden tables and benches. The toilets were located down some very narrow stairs and as I entered I felt uneasy, like someone was watching me. Checking my appearance out in the full length mirror I saw behind me, in my reflection an arch of white mist. It seemed to hang in the air around my head shoulders and waist. The more I stared in disbelief the thicker (or denser) the mist became. I did not panic, but left the bathroom sharply, slamming the bathroom door firmly closed behind me, shudders running up and down my spine. I climbed those narrow stairs rather quickly and must have looked pale as I re-entered the shop; my friends asked me if I had seen a ghost!
I am very open to most things and do not believe or disbelieve, but I know what I experienced. Did I see something behind me which you can explain? Was it 'spirit energy? Or a ghost?

Lisa, Suffolk

Dominic's Reply:

I'm sure the last thing on your mind that morning was anything 'paranormal'. You did not go out looking for ghosts, in fact the opposite; all you wanted was to have a few hours shopping with your friends. This makes your experience even more compelling. Old buildings like you described can hold many secrets, just think of all the people who have come and gone over the years. The old wooden benches and tables, the narrow staircase leading down to what was in the past more than likely the seller, now the 'washrooms' would have some tales to tell if they could talk. Ideal ground to encounter 'replay' ghosts. The theory is that old buildings built of stone and wooden construction can absorb the energy of the people who once lived and worked there. This energy can be stored inside the structure of the building for centuries, trapped just waiting for the right atmospheric conditions to trigger its release. Your description of an 'arch of white mist' is a classic way of describing, 'ectoplasm'. This is more commonly seen in séances and is claimed to be 'spirit energy' which a medium could produce. This is normally from the mediums mouth in evidence to support a claim of the afterlife being present in the room. Though this is yet to be proved or disproved as mediums were prone to faking the appearance of this substance.

What you saw in the mirror was no doubt real. You could have just been in the right place at the right time when all the factors aligned, releasing this 'white mist' or ectoplasm, falling right for you to see it. Was it a ghost? Just because something happens which cannot be explained by science does not make it 'paranormal', what you saw was rare but it may not be a ghost. To be a ghost it has to have senescence or intelligence which can indicate free will. This mist did not display any signs of free will.

Question:

Could you help me with understanding something that has happened to me? Each day I catch the train to work, different day same routine, one day is much the same as the next. Two days ago I had a dream I would meet a man on the train, the dream was clear and distinct. Being of rational mind I thought it was just another dream until to my great surprise I saw the exact same man on my train staring directly at me from across the carriage. Just like my dream. I recognised him in an instant.

He was tall, about six foot, dark brown eyes, which I felt were just looking directly through me. At first we just looked at each other, neither one daring to speak. Then he smiled and came over to where I was sitting. "You look familiar" he said, whilst writing his number on a piece of paper, "call me", my name is James. As I was already running late and the train had just arrived at my station I had no time to think, so I snatched the piece of paper and pushed it into the top of my handbag. I was so excited and could hardly think of anything else all day. The moment I got home from work I went to put his number into my phone and to my amazement it was already there! It had been in my phone for two years! When I tried to phone James, the number had been disconnected. This is a real mystery and I'm not sure what to do next. Can you explain what has just happened please?

Natasha. London.

Dominic's Reply:

There may be more than one explanation for what you experienced. But first we must explore the possibility that your dream was a premonition. Because we are taught time is a straight line, starting when you were born and moving forward till you pass over to spirit. The concept of seeing future events happening before they happen in a 'premonition' can go against how we think of time. But what other explanation is there? Well you could have gone backwards in time. What is not in dispute is that you met this man on a train and exchanged phone numbers. The only thing which has to be worked out is 'when' did it happen in the past, present or future? Could you have experienced a 'time slip'? Very likely. (A time slip is when a person finds for no apparent reason they are in a different time, either past or future.) Putting all the pieces together it might have worked like this. First in the present you had your premonition of meeting this man in your dream. An event you had yet to experience.

You stepped on that train and were drawn back in time. Met your man as predicted, exchanged phone numbers. Got off the train went to work and thought no more of it. On arriving home you went to put his number in your phone and discovered you had already placed his number in your phone two years previously. Because your meeting had only just happened because of the time slip, you had no memory of having met James or adding his number to your phone. Hence when you tried to phone him the number was no longer in use. Time slips are rare but not undocumented. People have been drawn backwards in time and seen future events happening only to find themselves in the present and confused. As I said, these events are rare and often offer no evidence to support the person's claims. In your case you have your mobile phone record which supports your account. I'm just sorry you did not get to know this man again.

Question:

Not sure if this is a medical or spiritual related question. I am smelling a cigarette smell at the moment which is horrible as I don't smoke. No one else can smell it. I've also noticed my eyes are stinging a bit as well, as if there is smoke around....I have had problems with smoking spirits around me before, (really heavy smokers as well!), but this is a lot lighter. Still annoying and constant too! Do you think this is spirit around me? Can spirit make us smell and hear them? If so how is this achieved? As a medium do you have any thoughts on who it is please and why are they here?
Thanks in advance.

Louise Surrey

Dominic's Reply:

What we have to understand with spirit is that every single thing they do is done by thought or the energy of thought. Spirit manifest what they want to create this way. It is very likely you are being made aware of 'spirit' by spirit putting their thoughts directly into your consciousness. This is why you are able to smell and even taste the cigarettes with your own senses.

You have stated this is becoming uncomfortable, so simply request through your thoughts for them to stop. Spirit will never go against your own personal will or wellbeing. It is worth knowing mediums will use their five senses when working with spirit. I will often receive messages with certain tastes or smells which confirm the person is who they say they are. Cigarette smoke, the taste of sugary foods can be common, as are certain perfumes and after shaves. (Mediums will seldom wear any scent or eat before working, just in case it interferes with the sitting.) I think of this as confirmation of the link between the two sides of life when spirit transfer the memory of a sense into the actual sensation. The difficulty we have is understanding the transformation of 'thoughts' into senses. You have learnt this skill without being aware of your ability to receive such messages through your five senses. As for working out who they might be could be anyone's guess. Because you are in receipt of the communication directly from 'spirit' yourself, it might be an idea just to ask. If you want to. Be open with yourself when the answer comes back. You may be surprised. A guide or a long lost relative could be wanting to get your attention, or just simply make you aware of their closeness to you.

Question:

How do I open up my sixth sense? My intuition is good and I'm learning how to sense spirit but I still do not know who is there, even though I know someone is! I get the sensation of a cobweb touching my face and hair, my whole body feels like it has electricity gently running through it on both sides. I would like very much to develop my ability so I can be sure that spirit is close. Any tips, hints or suggestions which could help me progress in the right direction please?

Philip. Liverpool

Dominic's Reply:

Interesting how you ask about your 'sixth' sense. This is your first sense, the most natural of all the senses once you rediscover how to connect. The key to opening up your intuitive sense is to use your other five senses to help you. First we must consider what 'Spirit' is. It is my belief that 'spirit' is pure thought, it is only when we are mortal we have five extra senses.

So when 'spirit' comes close this may allow them to experience the same sensations as they did when mortal, through us. We can use this knowledge to learn to recognise the signs of spirit. Train your mind to understand the different flavours of taste. How do you know what a certain food tastes of when your eyes are closed?

Because 'spirit' may only have a memory of certain flavours 'spirits' close by will help you pick up the description through their memory. This takes practice but is a great way of knowing how close the spirit world really is. Psychometry (touch) is brilliant at connecting you. But do not use your hands, your feet are the most sensitive part of your body, try walking bare footed into a building, the energy will pour in through your feet. First impression only and keep it simple. Learn how to see 'Auras' your sight is a valuable sense, in my book 'Aura Life in 4 D' I explain how to see 'Auras' using a dark background. This will open up this sense to a whole new world of understanding bringing you closer to your 'spirit guides'.

Question:

Past lives have intrigued me all of my life. I'm sure the reason for this is I still see and feel things that are strangely familiar but have no relevance in my current life. Could it be we hold on to memories from previous life times?

Could there be signs which I would recognise? I experience dreams which feel very real, but that is all they are 'dreams'. I would like to be able to recall these images in another way, maybe hypnosis? But as I know nothing about this I am concerned about how safe it is. I do not want to bring back into my consciousness any difficult 'past life' memories.

I'm drawn to India, the culture, language and even the food. Could this be I have a subconscious knowledge of that country from living there? How do I explore the possibilities?

Amy. Stoke

Dominic's Reply:

It is very possible your dreams are recalling events of previous life times' spent in India. Certain triggers can bring these memories to the surface of your consciousness. No matter how many life times your soul has experienced certain things will remain the same. Emotions, the sun, the sky, the need for sleep, water, food and warmth, these will all be familiar to each individual life you have lived. Memories lock inside your soul from previous lives. Known as 'soul memories'. Your past life memories will be reawakened by experiencing in your current life something feeling familiar. This is why you have an affinity with the culture of India without ever having been there. It is enough just to recognise this part of yourself whilst knowing it is more than just an over active imagination. You mention the dreams you are experiencing. If possible keep a dream diary, this will help you match up your dreams to the transcript of your regression; so if you wish to research your previous lives you will have some information to start with.

Hypnosis is a safe and easy way to access your 'soul memory'. Your starting point is to find a registered hypnotherapist. Your local doctors would keep a list of qualified hypnotherapists in your area. I have performed over 200 past life regressions with no after affects. The information received is often of significant understanding which helps the person resolve long standing issues or phobias which affected their lives.

Question:

Can an animal or the spirit of an animal 'haunt' a building? If the answer is 'yes', how could the animal's spirit be moved over to 'The Spirit World?' Would this be different to helping the spirit of a person? I would also like to know how the 'Spirit World' is for animals, do they share the same realm as people? Or do they have their own separate worlds? Am I right just to think of 'The Spirit World' as an extension of this world, with all creatures' great and small living together?

Alice. Kent

Dominic's Reply:

Animals have souls and are sentient. It is very possible for the energy of an animal to remain on Earth, especially if they are taken without warning. There are some very endearing accounts of dogs and cats wanting to remain by their owner's side, even after the animal has passed. The process of moving an animal spirit on is much the same as it would be for a person. The common link is 'love'. Animals are far easier to reach than people because animals have unconditional love. Thought is the same for animals as for humans, moving a 'spirit' over is about linking in to the thought process gently so as not to frighten the spirit. (Animal or human.) Once this link has been established then the transition can be made with direct communication (thought to thought) allowing for a smooth ascendance into the world of spirit.

The 'Spirit World' is not an extension of this mortal world. In my belief thought creates the surroundings for all sentient life. You choose your own existence, this would be the same for animal and humans. So it is very possible that animals choose how they want to live. If we can separate the 'mortal' from the 'spirit world' it helps us to understand the concept of 'manifestation' (thought becomes things), which applies to every living soul.

Your Questions

I hope you enjoyed reading my answers to some very intriguing questions. If you have any questions of your own please feel free to contact me on my e-mail address at the end of this book. I promise to answer all questions which have an e-mail or reply address attached.

Changing

I forget who answered to the question – "How do we change the World"?
"By random acts of kindness, one at a time." But I liked their answer.
Nothing grand or difficult, just random acts. Something which we are all capable of doing. Looking out for others, holding doors open, a friendly smile, a warm welcome. All acts of kindness. But something else happens when you re-align your attitude with kindness, you feel better. This is the boomerang effect. Everything starts and ends with us.
This is not always easy. Moods come and go, people can be difficult, but as I found out the other night by just engaging a person in conversation new ways of thinking can be born in an instant.

CHAPTER THIRTEEN

Hindsight

Lessons

If life has taught me anything it has taught me that everything comes to an end. Sometimes by choice and sometimes by the order of life. This understanding has changed my attitude to life, tomorrow does not matter, it is this moment that counts.

Every single day is packed full of opportunities to show, share and improve.

The terrible events of 9/11 brought home to me the value of life. On that morning so many people left for work, a normal day, quick kiss goodbye and gone. No time to stop, no time to consider.

The minutes before the planes hit the twin towers those souls on board had time to think. They knew those moments would be short, just enough time to say goodbye. My heart goes out to all who experienced those dreadful minutes. How do you ever come to terms with such sadness?

Put yourself in that position,

You only have ten minutes left to live, you have you mobile phone and a chance to call anyone in your address book. Who would you call?

I let you think for a moment, now what are you waiting for? Call them now.

There are not many moments when we stop to consider who means what to us. You can go a life time without letting those who are close to us know what they mean to us.

I was never given the chance to understand this when I was growing up. My life changed at a rapid rate, not much chance to stop and consider. Survival is more important than gathering knowledge.

Roll Models

Your first role models in your current life are your parents.

Being spiritual I believe we choose the parents we wish to be born to. Looking back I would have been a different person if the family I had been born into had been different.

As a child I felt responsible for everything. I had no concept of being a child, my own personal needs never counted. Expectation was placed upon me without reward, only punishment. I learnt that if I behaved I would be left alone, if I challenged or looked for attention I would be punished. Behave or else! Crazy, thinking back, because the whole process of growing up is one where we need help, love and understanding. Care free days, which should be the happiest days, not the days that you feel you should be seen and not heard.

I still struggle to forgive my mother and father for their ignorance, self-indulgence and pure lack of empathy. With hind sight I understand so much more about them as people. I realise just how little they did for me because they struggled to do anything for themselves.

My spiritual beliefs stem from my very early days, if I did ask for this life, choose my parents, and their circumstances then I have made a right mess of understanding this. It has taken me fifty years to even consider forgiveness, and I'm still not there, though I now understand everything starts with 'self', including forgiveness.

Change

How I feel about myself has changed so much in thirty five years. If I could have written to my 20 year old self, this is what I might have said.

Letter to self

Dear Dominic,

I hope you get the chance to read this, I may not be able to get you to listen. I still have problems with understanding when to talk and when to listen. If you can master this skill it will certainly help you.

Try to understand others, empathy is a word you might not learn until it is too late. But if you understand tolerance you are half way there. Do not jump into new things too quickly, you may want to shift your life in a positive direction without realising that people do not always say what they mean. Those who offer friendship and companionship may have their own agendas which are invisible. Be careful in love.

Follow your passions, they will emerge whether you embrace them or not. It is not okay just to follow. You are unique. Just because you have never been told that as of yet doesn't mean that you're not.
Stay fit. You take your health for granted, that is never a good idea, and you could pay a price if you're not respectful of your body.

Finally, avoid conflict at all costs. There will be many who like you. A few that will not, no matter what you do.
Be happy, live each moment as if it does not matter, when it means everything.
See you in thirty five years,
Love
Dominic.

Backwards

Every day before I start my work I stop and think 'who am I going to meet today? The world is a wonderful place, crammed full of amazing people and experiences just waiting to be embraced. So why look backwards? Yes it is right to acknowledge where you have been, but you do not look over your shoulder when walking forward. I believe it is a mistake to live in the past. Forgiveness is not for others it is for yourself. Believe me this little gem of understanding has taken me a long time to realise.

If I am right there will always be time in the 'now' to mend any bridges. First you have to face yourself. I have found it easier to just avoid. Maybe this is what makes me the person I am today. I do not want to look back, just straight ahead. I will never know why people make the choices they do, there are times I struggle to understand my own choices! So why judge? The chances are I would never understand even if I knew everything about that individual. Like I said, I struggle to understand myself.

Regrets

I have no time for regrets, life is for the living. Spirituality is teaching me that the moment is all we have. The past is just that, though through my research on 'past lives' I believe it is very possible we can get caught in a loop, repeating the same 'life times', over and over again. If true we have no need to look back, we would get the opportunity to change the choices. Not many of us like the prospect of living the same life time over and over again. Once is hard enough. But if we listen to our soul, and I mean listen, then the mistakes would shout louder, after all the experience of any given situation especially the emotionally charged moments are going to be at the top of our soul memory. The familiarity, that sense of foreboding are often present when our instincts are fully activated. Ask yourself, 'how many times have you ignored your inner sense only to find it was correct once the situation had been completed? Yes, hind sight is an amazing thing, but what if we all possessed the memories of every life time we had ever lived? And some of those life times had been repeat lives, at our own request because we messed up? Or circumstances took us over to the realm of spirit before we had a chance to gather or fulfil our own purpose? The power of repeating a life time would make perfect sense. It may also go some way to explaining why in certain circumstances we feel that we had been here before.

This could be why I do not have regrets, the thought that if you do mess up, or make bad choices you are going to get another chance. Nothing is ever over, until you believe it to be. The lesson could be that we all live in our own individual realities, creating the life that we believe. Thought is ever powerful, ever present. Thought is the only constant link between the mortal body and the spiritual existence.

Reality

I am certainly coming to understand that it could be possible that we all create our own personal realities. Others respond to us how we believe they are going to. What we think and believe in is far more powerful than we may ever have imagined.

What I find incredible about this is everything, but nothing matters. You see if we have the ability to think or build anything, everything is possible, nothing is out of reach. It is just what we believe which stops or starts us. Each one of us can change everything or nothing. Belief is all we need. Not faith, not repeating or copying, just the knowledge that your life becomes what you create with your thoughts.

This philosophy makes so much sense to me. It stops me looking back and wishing times had been different. It also explains why the authorities are so keen to get hold of our young minds. The school system is designed to teach and reward those who comply with the way of thinking we are taught.

Breaking it down it goes like this; believe in God. Be loyal to the course, which ever course they teach. Do not question. By the age of six our thoughts are taught 'to do what we are told.' Ambition is to work hard enough to have the rewards of all the material possessions. Life style, money. Personal goals matter. Acquirement of wealth is a sign of success in life.

Once you understand this you then have choices. You can choose the way you are taught, follow the pathways which you are lead down, and live a life which has been designed for you, understanding that the reality you are living, the one which you follow is not yours, just presented to you as an easy option. No self-thought goes into this.

Society

The society in which we live, (from the spiritual aspect) is our choice to create our reality right here, right now. It is hard to avoid the rules and the ways of society. We must live in the times and follow the guidelines set out for us. This is our reality. It will never change until enough people change how they see their own personal realities.

Take money.

Money rules everything we do. It is easy to see how time equals money. This is the only way we have ever known life. A pecking order driven by academic achievement. Those who achieve academically earn more money. Those who achieve less have less money.

So how would it be if everyone did their work for free? Nothing had a price. Those who wished to study did so, those who wanted to pursue other options were allowed to. No class, just a place in society which suited the individual?

Everything was free, equal. You choose what life style you lead. No greed, or status.

This concept is so far removed from the way we think it sounds like the impossible dream. No hunger, no need. Everyone would have enough. No control, no crime, no leaders based on wealth. All because money was taken out of our realities.

It would not work!

No it wouldn't, not the way we are thinking at this time in history. It has taken many centuries of conditioning and control to get us to where we are today. But if we were able to change the way we think it would work. The reality we live in is the reality we choose to live with. Each one of us has the power within to change our own individual reality. By starting to see we are what we believe and think ourselves to be; it changes everything.

This chapter only touches briefly on 'thought and concepts of thoughts'. I like the idea that regrets are unnecessary. I would like to be right about repeating life times, I have met those who believe the same as me, that it is highly likely we do. It has occurred to me that thought and belief has everything to do with whether we experience or not. A paradox. Let me end on a thought given to me by a friend I was lucky enough to spend some time with.

Last Word

I could never get my thoughts around astrology. How could the planet dictate who we are? Surely the whole of the Earth's population could not be divided by twelve? Then how about Pluto and planet x? (Planet x is the one missing planet in our solar system scientists believe exists but has never been proven until recent times.) Pluto has been downgraded to a dwarf planet in the last ten years.

Surely as our knowledge grows the charts change? This would then put in question the whole concept which astrology was founded on.

My astrological friend was having none of this. His answer was clear and well considered.

And I quote, "Whatever is in the human collective consciousness is what effects the charts, if we believe that Pluto is a full size planet then it is." "Planet x has not be found so it has no effect on the charts." In other words we have to believe it to be so before it can be so.

CHAPTER FOURTEEN

Believe

Being remarked upon is the only way to be noticed. Not my words, but true enough. When others talk about you it says more than you could ever say about yourself.

This is why I like to experience firsthand for myself.

This next story is something so strange that if I had not seen it with my own eyes I would not have believed it. This is the first time I have written about that cold November day back in 1977.

November 1977

Like all school days I only ever used to look forward to games. Nothing else just Physical Education. At fourteen years old I was fit, a lot fitter than many in my school. I put this down to the fact that each day before school I would get up at 6.00 am to do a paper round. This was something I would do without question for four years. Delivering newspapers seven days a week had the effect of keeping me well above the average level of fitness for my age. It also resulted in me being first in the cross country races, quicker to the ball in hockey, football and captain of the school basketball team.

I would pack my sports kit with expectation twice a week and climb the hill outside our house to catch the school bus without complaint.

I can remember this November day was a sports day, I had two bags to carry, both straps crisscrossed over my chest, hanging one bag on each hip.

The journey to school was boring, the coach had to pick up children from the surrounding villages, and this would take much longer than necessary. The older children would sit on the back seat and smoke, whilst the fumes would make me feel sick. I could not wait to get off.

This day was the same as any other, first port of call would be my locker situated in the long school corridor which linked all the classrooms, staff room and head teachers office.

My school was modern, built in the sixties to educate the children of the local area. What a mix there was, as the local area was farm land, an Army camp, and the brand new privately owned housing estate I lived on. It was a tough school, with tough children. Fights were common, discipline harsh. Punishment by cane, or slipper would be an everyday occurrence, often for stupid little things like walking up the wrong side of the stairs, or eating in class.

The classrooms were light and airy, large metal framed windows would light up the rooms, but the gaps would freeze the life out of you on cold winter days.

Reaching my locker on the ground floor, I could hear a commotion in the classroom. I hurried to place my sports kit inside the flimsy metal box, and rushed to see what all the fuss was about.

Peering around the half opened door I could see a group of about twenty children all looking at the last but one window. The level of noise was loud as the excited chatter of what they were looking at came into focus.

Condensation

The window (approximately one foot by three foot) had steamed up, the condensation had an image etched into it of a devil. A little imp like character, with menacing eyes, six pack stomach, and tiny horns protruding from its forehead.

To me it looked like it had been stenciled onto the window, but in fact was created by the moisture drying in certain areas and leaving the condensation untouched to create a three dimensional image. No runs or smudges. Just the image of what looked like the devil.

To my fourteen year old self it was remarkable. Even the teachers were astonished and could not offer an explanation.

Unique

When you are young how can you appreciate seeing something that was unique? You have nothing in your understanding to compare this to. It could be something that just happens on a regular basis, windows could form images all the time. (I remember my mother telling me as a small boy that 'Jack Frost' had visited during the night when the windows in my bedroom would freeze on the inside.) Or something so rare that the likelihood of you seeing something similar again in your life time unlikely.

This was the latter. I have never ever seen anything like this since. I haven't read of anyone talking about any similar experience of seeing an image on the inside of a window.

It could be that since those day of cold metal framed windows schools and houses are far better insulated. Heating systems retain the heat in buildings, windows do not steam up anymore.

I believe with hind sight and knowledge the event I witnessed that November morning was rare. Images of the devil do not appear every day. I was privileged to see it.

I have also considered the possibility of the whole thing being a practical joke. I have thought about how difficult it would be to get such a perfect image, no runs, no smudges, just a clear crisp portrait. It would be difficult to recreate, and I have tried with stencils and hairdryers, I have come nowhere near recreating what was on that window.

Logical

I have to admit I have no logical explanation. I am not saying there might not be a way to explain, just that I haven't been able to.

The paranormal is just that, a subject or experience which cannot be explained. Something has happened which has no way of fitting into what we currently accept to be true.

I have since heard it said that the devil shows itself somewhere different every day. Could it be on that particular day it chose my school?

Very possible, when you think the reason to show yourself is to be remarked upon, and to make an impression. Where better than a school with impressionable children?

The image has stayed with me for forty years.

The Hall

I get invited to various locations from time to time. Many hotels, public houses and homes which make claims of being haunted. I would go as far as saying most are not. Hotels and public houses like the publicity and will hold ghostly events to get the till filling up. Profit or greed are behind most ghost sightings.

As you might have gathered I am no fan of these establishments. This next story is true and the events are as written. I would like you, the reader, to work out for yourself what the motivation was behind charging people more than enough to walk around an old country house in the middle of the night.

Invite

I had received an e-mail inviting me to a country house in the middle of the countryside. The 'Most Haunted' television show would be filming over a couple of days and would like it if I could attend.

Since I had left 'Ghost-House' the previous year I had not been involved in the pursuit of ghosts. I found the whole commercial thing a little distasteful.

But having worked with a few of the 'Most Haunted' team at 'Ghost House' I had accepted. I was told in advance the public would be paying to visit and part of my duties (unpaid) would be to walk a group around the house. In exchange I would be welcome to join in, eat and drink as much as I liked.

Evening

The house looked splendid in the late autumn evening light. The film crew had set up and the presenters had all been busy recording their pieces to camera.

My friend, who was one of the main historians on the programme had greeted me with his wife and the show's medium. I knew them all, having worked with them all at some time.

It was good to see them, time passes so fast and you get to make friends you may not see for months.

The shows medium and I had recently finished filming a psychic television programme in Berlin, Germany. We got on very well; so when he told me about room 7 I could not help but be curious.

Room 7

Apparently this house had a very special room. The reason the television crew had come down to the house was this 'Room 7'. They had been told by the people who looked after the house that room 7 was haunted by the ghost of a man who had committed suicide, the room was so badly cursed it had been locked up for over seventy years with no one allowed in under any circumstances. 'Most Haunted' would be the first people to step inside the room in over seventy years. The room should be a time capsule, covered in dust. The owner of the house had been very pensive about allowing the film crew in and had made them all sign disclaimers in the case of something bad happening.

The grand opening of room 7 was to be the climax of the hour long programme.

Exciting

I was really looking forward to the evening, just one thing left to do and that was take a tour of the house myself. I never liked leaving anything to chance and the house itself was large enough to get lost in, if not prepared.

I asked one of the volunteers who worked at the house to take me around for my own personal tour before the public arrived.

A nice middle aged lady, who told me she was a teacher by day and a volunteer by night. She had been working at the house for six years, and although being present at a lot of these events she had never seen anything. A little disappointing she told me as we walked off together to explore the back lengthy corridors.

The sun was now just dipping below the horizon, and the house became hidden behind the shadows of the tall trees which lined the ground around the gravel car park and long drive way.

The front of the house was grand, large rooms with very high lights hanging from the middle of the magnificent ceiling roses. You could feel the history as you walked past each room and up the wide rosewood stair case.

I wanted to go round the back of the house, the part the public would not normally visit, and the corridor that led to room 7.

Taking a sharp right, then a left, the lady showed me through a tiny storage room, covered with dust sheets and stacks of chairs, "here we are", she said, the back passage way.

Now the light was dim, but not black. In the gloom a tall gentleman with a top hat, black dinner jacket and grey trousers walked straight towards us. I looked at the lady, she looked at me and the figure walked right through us both.

It was one of those moments when you know what you have seen, but struggle to believe it.

There was no doubt, we had both just witnessed the same man. I was a little surprised, the volunteer was ecstatic. "First time in six years I have ever seen anything." She exclaimed in an excited voice, still in a state of shock.

All I could think was 'fantastic' if this place can do this we are going to have a great night.

We made our way back down the stairs, not so grand at the back of the house, saw room 7, to which the lady gave me one of those knowing looks, almost to say, you will not be disappointed. A large notice on the door written in rather neat small writing, simply said, 'keep out'.

I could not wait until the end of the evening, I just wanted to walk in right then.

Public

We made our way back to the main entrance. By now crowds of people had arrived, all chatting energetically. People had cameras, meters to measure temperature, dowsing rods and most of all big smiles. Everyone was looking forward to a night of ghost hunting.

I had a quick word with my friend, the medium and just pointed out what we had seen in the back passage, it was only right, I wanted the television crew to capture on camera what I had witnessed, it would make the programme popular, and could prove beyond doubt the existence of ghosts.

We both came to the same conclusion that what we had seen was a reply ghost, most likely triggered by the energy and the light going down that evening.

Meeting

I was just about to take my group, when the medium who had held the fake séance at 'Ghost House' two years before caught my eye. "Hello again" he said. I must have turned white with shock!

He continued. "What do you think of the house?" "Not as good as Ghost-House" I said with a smile and made my excuses. Meeting this medium again worried me, I knew he was not who he claimed to be and if anything was going to go wrong it would be something to do with him. But benefit of any doubt, must be given. But I did feel slightly uneasy.

The tour went well, uneventful, but those who brought cameras caught some orbs, questions were answered and the people were happy.

The replay ghost in the back corridor did not show himself again, but I was pleased for the volunteer. A moment to remember for her.

Now for room 7

Anti-Climax

This moment had to be reserved for the shows historian and medium. I watched on from the side of the door, through the lens of the camera man. The crew had a night vision camera, and a static camera with sound and lighting set up. The buzz of expectation fell silent as the key was turned in the door. The two men entered room 7, the first people to step inside for seventy years.

The atmosphere was tense, that is until the historian decided to try the light switch, click, and the room lit up! Rather odd, then looking around the dusty room, a desk with draws in came into view.

Deciding to look inside, the first draw revealed a newspaper, dated 1992. The whole story had been made up.

I was not at all surprised, my instincts had been on guard ever since I saw that fake medium in the entrance. Everyone was disappointed, the climax to this episode would have to be something else. The ghost in the corridor would fit the bill.

The lady volunteer was only too happy to share her story, demonstrating with expressive hands and face gestures, as she replayed her encounter with a 'replay ghost'.

The production team did a good job in recreating the ghost of the gentleman in the top hat and evening jacket, in a mock up to demonstrate the ghost of the back passage.

Friends

It is always nice to see friends. Much of the work as a psychic medium is done alone. The best part of working for yourself is I get to choose who I work with, good or bad but I always look for the good in everyone.

CHAPTER FIFTEEN

Life Before Life

Here are some true stories about past life regression.

My office phone rang, instinctively I reach out and lift the receiver, "Hello" I don't want any of that tarot card nonsense said a very distinctive west midlands accent! "That's alright then, I said because I don't read tarot over the phone" The lady's name was Gail, and there was something in her voice which just cried out for help. From the very first moment Gail spoke, I didn't know whether or not I could help her, sensing her plight was a difficult one, but I just knew we would be friends forever.

Gail was in a relationship with a man who was to say the least difficult to understand. He would be easy going, charming, a wonderful person. Gail had fallen for him the moment she set eyes on him. They moved in together, a small flat, so very much in love, when Gail gave birth to a little boy their life was complete. Gail loved her child more than life itself, but the relationship with the father was going downhill, he would still be charming to everyone outside his family, but would fail to help with the child, often going out for days on end, he would accuse Gail of being unfaithful checking all her movements. For some reason he couldn't cope with being a father. Gail and her son grew close and by the time they brought their first house together the relationship was failing, Gail was unhappy, feeling trapped. The lack of trust between them was killing the relationship. They would have massive fights, huge arguments. He would threaten her that if she ever left him for another man he would kill her and their son. By the time I got to speak with Gail, her life had reached crises point, she could no longer live the life he wanted her to live. With great courage she threw him out, no longer being able to cope with his paranoid behaviour. He went to live at his mothers. Gail now alone with her son was able to allow herself some breathing space, her partner was still in the background, his double personality still very much in evidence, threatening phone calls would be followed by other calls stating his undivided love for her.

During this time Gail's thoughts had turned to another man and although they were just friends Gail was starting to fall for him, without knowing it she was falling in love with another man, he was kind, gentle and above all got on well with her son.

Realisation

Then a bomb shell dropped. This man who was becoming more than just a friend in Gail's own mind, decided to move overseas. Again Gail was devastated, she was still getting mixed messages from her ex-partner who had settled into a routine at his mothers, but still wouldn't accept that Gail didn't want him. He would do his best to persuade her he was a changed man and how it would work if he moved back home with the two of them.

After a long summer holding out, she decided to try again with her partner. He moved back home and they hoped for another child, Gail had always wanted a little girl.

But yet again things were going to change on a sixpence.

In late December of the same year her partner was taken ill, admitted to hospital, and died.

Gail was inconsolable, alone, and her life in pieces all over again. Her partner was dead, and the man she had fallen in love with was many thousands of miles away.

Time Past

Six months on and Gail was struggling to rebuild her life, her weight had dropped alarmingly. It was at this stage she asked me to regress her to see if we could find the answers to why in this life she had been taken down this road. Had her partner been with her before? Why did she fear losing her child? Why did she feel so much love for this man overseas?

What follows is a trans-script of the session Gail went through, hoping to find those answers.

I started by taking Gail into the space between lives to see what she would recall.

Gail's session starts -

What do you see?
DARK
How do you feel?
SCARED, THERE IS A LONG CORRIDOR IN FRONT OF ME, I SEE MIST A BUILDING AT THE END WITH AN ARCHWAY.
What do you see under the archway?
AN OLD MAN, HE HAS A BEARD, HE WANTS ME TO DECIDE.

Decide?
DECIDE ON MY OWN FATE

(I believe this means that the man wants Gail to decide on the course of her next life time. This fits because the reality we decide to live is the reality we have chosen.)

Are you still walking?
YES, I'M NOW IN A COURT YARD, IT'S A CIRCLE, WITH COBBLES ON THE GROUND, AND A WELL IN THE CENTER. THERE ARE FIELDS WITH LONG GRASS.
What are you wearing?
LONG DRESS, WHITE APRON...
Are you still walking?
NO
What do you see?
A BIG ROUND TABLE. ONE CHAIR, 7 MEN WITH DARK HAIR. LONG RED AND BLUE ROBES.
HEALING ENERGY, FEEL CALM.

Answers

The whole point of being regressed is to understand, not what happens after you passed to the realm of spirit, but what you have experienced previously during other life times. Just the fact you can recall detail such as the clothing you wore or the food you ate are significant. No past life is real until you can trace the origin. As records have been kept since the sixteen hundreds, you can look back through the history books. Full names, towns, locations are all good evidence.

This next piece is trying to establish some more detail, facts, dates and names.

What year is it?
1810
How do you feel?
DO NOT LIKE THIS
Do not like?
CRUEL TO ME
Who is?

MY HUSBAND, HE HITS ME.
How old are you?
25
How long have you been married?
1 YEAR
Where do you live?
SMALL HOUSE IN THE MIDDLE OF A TOWN.
Do you know the name of the town?
NO

(This is all well and good but no hard information is forth coming from Gail. I try a new line of questioning in the hope more 'researchable' information is revealed.)

Do you have children at this stage of your life?
BABY GIRL, ONE LITTLE BOY.
MY FRIEND WILF WORKS IN THE FIELDS, GENTLE, CANNOT HAVE HIM.
MY DAUGHTER IS WILF'S

(This is the first time that Gail has revealed a name 'Wilf' I can now try for more names.)

What are you going to do?
TAKE CHILDREN AND GO. HUSBAND DOESN'T KNOW. SCARED HE MIGHT FIND OUT.
What is your husband's name?
WILLIAM, BILL
What is his job?
WORK'S WITH HORSES
Do you know where you live?
A SMALL VILLAGE BY THE SEA. IN THE COUNTY OF SUFFOLK.

(Now I have established another name and the location is becoming closer.)

Are you in danger?
YES...
Why?
HUSBAND KEEPS HITTING ME.

FEEL SLEEPY.

(At this stage Gail was very distressed so I decided to take her forward to her next life. Not much information, but might be able to trace the names or location.)

I move forward in time.

What is the year?
1912
Who are you?
A LITTLE GIRL, FEEL HAPPY... LOOKING FOR MUM AND DAD. FOUND MUM CAN NOT FIND DAD.
What is your mum's name?
PETRA

(Good start not a common name.)

When were you born?
BORN 1907
What is your name?
PETRA, SAME AS MY MUM'S. MY DAD'S DEAD. DAD WAS OLD. I'M A SECRET FROM DAD'S FAMILY.
What does your mum look like?
MUM HAS BLOND HAIR, WAVES, EVERYTHING MAKES ME LAUGH.
What country do you live in?
HOLLAND

(Language being spoken by Gail is still English?)

I want to move you forward now Petra, you are now at your thirteenth birthday, what do you see?
MY UNCLE ALF, HE IS MY MUM'S BROTHER, TALL, HIS EYE'S SMILING, I PLAY WITH HIM.
What is Alf wearing?
DARK UNIFORM TWO ROWS OF BUTTONS, HE DOESN'T ALWAYS WEAR UNIFORM
What does Alf look like?
TALL, DARK HAIR, WHISKERS ON HIS FACE. MAKES ME LAUGH. PICKS ME UP MOVES HIS WHISKERS UP AND DOWN NECK. ALF PLAYS WITH ME IN THE FIELD. I FEED THE HORSES

HE HAS TWO HORSES. FRIGHTENED, FAR TOO BIG. ONLY RIDE WHEN ALF IS THERE.

Petra can you tell me how your hair looks?

LONG BLOND

Where are you now?

IN THE FIELD

Are you with the horses?

YES I'M FEEDING THEM, THERE IS SOMEONE WATCHING ME,

Who?

NOT SPOKEN WITH HIM

What is he wearing?

WHITE SHIRT, HANSOM. MY UNCLE ALF IS VERY PROTECTIVE OF ME, LOVE MY UNCLE,

I'm going to move you forward, your now 25 years old.

Where are you?

AT HOME

Who is with you?

EDWARD, UNCLE ALF NOT PLEASED.

Is anyone else with you?

YES

Could you tell me who?

ROBERT

Who is Robert?

HE IS MY BABY ROBBIE, CHUBBY FACE MAKES ME SMILE

Who is the father?

EDWARD

Do you love him?

YES AND HE LOVES ME, BUT HE COMES AND GOES, I DO LOVE HIM

I'm now going to move you forward to the time you went over to spirit, how old are you?

35

Is Edward and Robbie still with you?

YES

Do you have any more children?

NO

WISH UNCLE ALF COULD SEE ROBBIE, HE DIED, ROBBIE LOOKS JUST LIKE HIM

How is Edward?

NOT GOOD HE DOESN'T LIKE ME, HE GOES WITH OTHER WOMEN. NO GOOD TO ME. SCARED NOBODY WILL LOOK AFTER ROBBIE

Why?

I'M DYING T.B BAD CHEST, SO SCARED DON'T WANT TO LEAVE ROBBIE.

(This final piece of the transcript has more information, names and places. But still struggling to get hard facts.)

Enough

At this stage I bring Gail out of her trance, but before she leaves she tries to hold onto Robbie I bring her out. The session has lasted just over an hour and a half.

The session has revealed why Gail has a fear of leaving her son in this life time, and the fact she has died young twice in her past two incarnations, once at the hand of her partner.

In her current life her partner was abusive but more with threats, intimidation, etc. rather than psychical violence.

The one big difference being he had died young, this time round leaving Gail to pick up the pieces, whereas in the previous lives Gail was the one who had died.

I believe she now has a chance to rebuild with her son, the life she should have had. Only time will tell whether or not she will be successful, but if she draws on the knowledge she now possesses it will only help her conquer the inner most fears that lie deep down.

There is no conclusion to Gail's story at the moment, because hers is a real life and she is living through what are ever changing times. But like I said at the beginning she will always be my friend.

Next Story

A man who I helped was so afraid of flying he would rather cross the Atlantic by boat than get on a plane.

America

He lived in America, his family in the UK, so every year he would make the long journey to see his parents, brothers and sister. If he could only just get on that plane life would be so much easier, but his phobia held a strong strangle hold over him. Petrified with irrational fear just at the thought of stepping on the staircase attached to the plane.

(We are all born with two fears or phobias; a fear of water, and a fear of heights. It's normal to have these naturally inborn instincts which go back to the time when we needed to survive. If we had fallen into water, or leaped off cliff tops we would have died, so inborn phobias serve a common purpose in all of us, and without them the human race wouldn't have evolved so fast. All other fears are either learned behaviour, i.e. being stung by a wasp as a child, we learned to fear wasps. Or something from a past life locked so deep in our memories that it takes regression through hypnosis to access.)

During past life regression I believe we access our 'Cell Memory'. This is our personal memory of everything we have ever experienced through every life we have lived.

This record is stored in the DNA of every cell in our bodies; a record of all the knowledge and lessons life has taught us throughout our existence. Soul memory (which is far deeper set in the memory) of life between lives. Our record of what happens to us whilst in spirit.

Fears

This man was genuinely in need of help; his fears, real to such an extent he had altered his life to avoid having to deal with the situation. He was now prepared to do whatever it took to rid him of this paralyzing condition.

I could hear my voice softly echo around the small room, "I want you to focus, only on my voice, I don't want you to do anything except relax." I began, "close your eyes and trust in my voice to guide you." I had done this a hundred times before. I could sense the man sinking down further, until he was deep under the hypnotic trance. I could now regress him stage by stage, first through his current life, back through school, childhood, memories of his upbringing came flooding back, with a tide of emotion, one minute laughing, the next crying, moving along at a pace going back further; four years old, two years old, one, then back into his earliest memories in his mother womb, warm peaceful.
I could see he was at ease with the whole process. This was enough for his first time this deep under, so I brought him back up through the same stages until he was back in the room with me. (I would never take a client back into a previous life too soon, especially if they had never experienced hypnosis, people can have different reactions and I always like to see how they feel when coming out.)

Past life memories can be upsetting. The last thing I would want is a disorientated person with emotional fears surfacing for the first time in many years going out into the world alone to deal with their everyday routine.

Forward

So it was a week later the man returned, this time I could see he was looking forward to the session, much more relaxed, ready to explore whatever I could uncover from his deep subconscious memory.

He was very soon under, knowing what to expect helps, the only difference was this time he would be going back past this lifetime.

I knew it was the fear of flying which had brought him to me, and as he was only just turned 31 this gave me a time period of about 50 years to work with, since the first flight by the Wright brothers hadn't been until 1912 or there about. I knew this phobia was going to be based on a life time which was between those years.

So starting step by step I gradually moved him back in time, (in past life regression "time" is the only indicator people can relate to) I would like you to step back, let your mind guide your thoughts, I could sense him tensing up. Tell me what you are feeling?

His voice shallow and not that easy to hear he started "I'm flying, so much noise, I can hardly hear myself think."

How are you flying?

"Airplane."

"Can you describe the airplane you're in?

"Small with square wings, glass above my head. It is a fighter a world war two fighter"

What are you wearing?

I saw him look down at himself, almost in disbelief, he described the uniform of an American fighter pilot, right down to the hand gun and knife he wore in his flight suit. Other information was to follow, his name, rank, and squadron. This was good because now we had the information we needed to verify that this person actually lived and wasn't some sort of fantasy brought on by watching too many World War two movies. I brought him out of his trance.

Fears

I didn't want him to relive the one thing he feared, it wasn't necessary, research would fill in the missing pieces.

He had been under for well over two hours. Sessions only ever lasted an hour; for many reasons, but mainly because we become over tired, this was the one exception, the evidence he had provided was, even for me, beyond belief.

I just had to follow up the story. But where to start, no better place than the service records of the American Air Force.

Photograph

And there he was, (even a photograph) a fresh young man with his service number. It transpired he had been shot down and killed whilst over the Atlantic! He was only 22 when he died.

He had been flying Mustangs (square winged fighter aircraft.) The date of his death, October 15 1943. Amazing proof of a life which he had lived some thirty years before, being born again into an English family.

Cemetery

The same year we went to visit The American War Cemetery. I was overwhelmed there, thinking of this young man who had been shot down defending his country.

He traced the family who were related to this World War Two flier. They still lived in Alabama and although his parents were dead, his brother and two sisters, (now in their early sixty's) children and grandchildren all attended.

Touch

I still get letters from time to time from him, explaining how he is now flying with no fear, he has two homes, one in America and one in England.

Seeing is believing. I've always wanted to experience because without you can listen to others, whilst relating to the teachings but you never know one hundred percent. All you can do is trust, because it's second hand.

To know something with all your heart are two opposites. The next two stories about past life regression were told to me second hand. I can't vouch for them personally, but having said that they are very interesting, in the same vein of the American Pilot, coming from a person whom I trust.

More past Lives

In India a small child knew far too much about his previous life time.

From the age of five the boy was convinced he had been the owner of a television shop in a city many miles away from where he now lived.

But what made this child's story stand out was in his account of this previous life he had been shot three times in the chest, and on the boy's chest were three 'round' birth marks, the same shape and size a bullet would have made.

Birth marks are often clues to how we might have died, in this child's case the details of his past life was remarkable. He knew his wife's name, and their children's names, he also described the front and insides of the shop in great detail. Of course his mother and father didn't believe him; how could their special little boy have been a completely different person in another life, so recent for him to remember everything.

As the boy grew he felt more and more compelled to visit the city where he knew he had lived and find his shop. This he did, to the total surprise of both his new and old family.

Shop

The outcome being he was able to convince his wife and children of who he really was, and now runs that very same shop! This is a very remarkable story, but I've learned past life stories can often be.

Clock

The second story which sticks in my mind is that of a man who lived in Canada in the 1970's.

He was an antique dealer, with a love of time pieces, clocks, and coins.

One particular clock (an old large gold and diamond carriage clock) had caught his eye in the window of a local jewellers. He felt it was familiar yet how could it be, the clock looked well over 90 years old? He knew it would be far out of his price range.

Cost

The man went about his normal daily routine but just couldn't get the carriage clock out of his thoughts, he would even dream about it, strange dreams where he would be sat around a table with people he had never seen before, celebrating.

The room was dimly lit with lots of old pictures on the walls, and the gold and diamond carriage clock on the mantelpiece above the fire

Was he going mad he asked himself? This dream was to continue with the people becoming like real figures in his mind; every day he would walk past the shop, the clock would sit there, looking at him, quietly ticking away, drawing his attention as if it had some hypnotic power.

Clear

He decided a doctor's visit was necessary, as he felt his life was being taken over by his clear visions of another time and place.

His doctor was not too sure what he could do for him, but he knew a colleague who specialized in past life regression.

So by a series of events he was sitting in this man's office, being taken deep down into a trance.

He was in the room he had seen in his visions, a large oblong shaped room with a large dining table. He was a young man, about 14 years old.

His whole family surrounded him. On his head a small cap (kippah.) He was Jewish; his whole family was. Looking around the room it was filled with valuable antiques and on the mantelpiece was the gold and diamond carriage clock, dimly lit in the flicking gas light.

The scene changed. He was now in his early twenties dressed in rags, painfully thin, no sign of his family, watching in horror as bodies were being thrown and kicked into a large trench.

He felt a sharp pain, then falling, falling so far, then the feeling of freedom, his last memories were of watching the souls of hundreds of people escaping upwards like firefly's being released from a jar.

He had lived before, the clock was a trigger to unlock these memories of a life as a Jewish man, who had died in the Holocaust.

After

The story goes that after being regressed he had told of his remarkable experience to the person who owned the jewellers, who in turn gave him back the clock. If true a fitting end.

This convinced me that past lives really do have an effect on our current life.

It is a progression of understanding, free will, fate and sometimes destiny that guides our very soul's existence.

Dominic - My own personal Regression Experience

My own past life regression reinforced my understanding of the subject, whilst studying I was given the opportunity to be taken back through a past life. Never being one to shy away or turn down a chance to learn something new about myself, I knew I just had to.

Hard Work

I can remember thinking you've got your work cut out with me!

Then I was under, awake but not awake, going back through my life, feeling the emotion of childhood, sitting in the doctor's waiting room, watching Katie run across the road, the fear of the footsteps outside my bedroom window, I felt very alone.

Then backwards into a warm safe feeling. I heard a voice pushing me back and back, where are you now it asked?

"I'm standing in the field, looking down I was dressed in heavy brown trousers, with braces, light blue shirt, reaching up to feel a cap.

I was a farmer, it was early spring, the year 1912, and to the amazement of my teacher I was talking French (a language that I had no previous knowledge of.)

So I was a French farmer in 1912.

Just Before

"I want to take you forward to the moment just before you passed into spirit"

"Where are you?"

I was in a trench the year was 1917 I was wearing the uniform of a French solider.

I was about to be bayoneted in the throat (even in this life my throat is my weak point)

I was killed in the battle for Ypres on the French/ Belgium border.

Name

Like all good past life regression the impressions given must be verified. Everything that came out that day was able to be backed up with facts, even my name, Dominique.

Future Life

So far I have shown some very impressive evidence on past lives, but what if we could go forward "Future Life Progression."

You already know my thoughts on time being a manmade structure which we order our lives with, who's to say what time is?

We turn the clocks back and forward each year, every fourth year we lose a whole day!! What is that all about?

It just goes to show how we manipulate time for our own ends.

Take this a step further, if time has no beginning or end it makes it a circle, so if we can go back in time, then we can also go forward.

That's where future life progression fits into the bigger picture. Now imagine going forward in your own life, what would you like to know?

It's a good question, because if we know what is coming up we can deal with any problems before they arise, life is no longer beyond your control.

Personally level

Let's think about future life progression on a world level. We are dealing with some really big issues. Just imagine what it would be like to take a glimpse of what the planet will be like in a hundred years' time.

Just the fact we could move forward is a positive message.

In my own personal experience of progression the people on Earth have learned to adapt to the ever changing climate. Homes are built underground, cars that run on water power, free energy from natural sources, microbes which eat rubbish, algae soaking up pollution. We have a bright future as a race, we have always taken up the challenge of survival, and the future is no different.

Lessons

So what can past or future lives teach us?

In a word, survival. The fact that the soul is eternal, and each and every one of us accountable for our own actions.

How we live, what we say, making choices right or wrong.

We are here to learn.

Life isn't set out in-front of us, we all have free will. We can do as we wish. I would find it too hard to believe some greater force could control our lives.

But having said that the choices we make start before we are born, certain pathways we wish to follow, experiences we choose to take, all decided upon before we start our new life.

Pathway

These will be placed along our journey if we decide or choose to take that pathway. When we pass over into the spirit world we are judged but not by anyone other than ourselves.

We all have our own personal journeys, some will take the quick route, and others will decide to take a slower pace. So whichever way we decided to play out our time here on Earth it pays to think positive, face any difficulties knowing that at some point we will overcome and move on, if not in our current life may be the next one.

One subject I haven't covered in this chapter so far is Shamanism.

All over the world for many centuries Shaman have been experiencing personal life journeys with the help of a natural drug called Iowasca.

Iowasca

Iowasca is in fact two different plants when brought together, the root of one and the leaves of another. When combined and boiled together in water they make a rich black tea which you drink; it tastes of bitter liquorice, and it is recommend that you don't eat for twenty four hours before you drink it, because if you have food in your system the Iosawsca will clear your body of that food before it starts you on your journey.

Stories

I have heard many stories told by people of their Iowasca journeys. People who have been met by strange creatures who have healed bad backs, broken limbs and so on. Because I have never experienced these beings for myself I keep an open mind on these claims. But I have been taken forward into a time and place I couldn't explain. Making me face my own personal fears. This is what happened.

Experience

I knew I wanted to do this, I had read so much about Iowasca, others explaining how it had changed their life, the journey into the subconscious mind. I had been told by a good friend of mine to relax and to allow, whilst going with the experience to where my journey took me.

I made sure no one would bother me for the next few hours, took the phone of the hook, drew the curtains, and in one large gulp swallowed a whole mug full of tepid bitter black liquid.

I felt sick, my head was spinning my mouth dry rough. I had expected all these feelings so I just relaxed making sure my body was in a comfortable position I laid down and closed my eyes.

At this stage I had no sense of time, so I didn't know how long it was before I felt a dream like state around my thoughts. I was in the desert, jet planes flying all around me,

I watched in horror as one plane was shot out of the air, black smoke bellowing from behind the aircraft, the pilot being thrown into the air, then drifting down slowly, his pale blue para-shoot silent in the still air. The noise was loud, people shouting and clapping firing guns up into the air celebrating.

The End

I was with a group of men, soldiers by the way they were dressed, I was living this experience, it was as though I had always been in this life, I slept eat and drank with the other men; we lived in an underground bunker built into the sand with blocks of stone and iron windows and doors.

I was fighting another war, but this time I was myself, in the desert.

Bunker

It was night now. I settled down in a metal framed bunk bed to get some rest, I felt uneasy, the air was tense and dry, and the other men were on edge.

I could hear loud explosions going off in the distance, jet planes roared overhead, I was scared.

Then a loud bang and shouting.

I saw a man I didn't recognises, I felt like my head had been hit by a large fist, then I came to, I was back in my room the sunlight shining though the gap in my curtains, I felt disorientated, my eyes couldn't focus my head painful my arms and legs stiff, I glanced towards my electric clock, it was 10 o'clock I had been under for over 12 hours!

Real?

What had I experienced?

I think I had seen my own death in this life, if ever there was a war in the desert I would make sure I was well away from it, I told myself. It was the summer of 1984 the first Gulf war was only 6 years away.

Looking back I believe what I saw was the end of my life, it was my biggest fear. I also believe the knowledge I gained saved my life, because I knew if I ever saw that bunker I would do all I could to escape.

Personal experience is everything and this was very personal and something that will stay with me always.

Thought

Nothing more whole than a broken heart. Most of us go through mind numbingly difficult personal relationships, or the loss of a close loved one. The pain which we feel as a mortal is way and above anything else we may encounter. I believe it is beneficial to share and show the hurt, but seldom come across those who are open enough. Even as a medium those who come have long and tall walls to first break down before being willing to show their ill-disguised emotions. Wouldn't it be the best if we could all let our hearts break so they could be mended? One day we may come to understand the soul is immortal and 'life after life' is the fate which awaits after we leave this mortal world.

CHAPTER SIXTEEN

Hero's

I want to talk about two people, one I have never met, and one that I share my life with. The first has talked about his life with refreshing honesty, the second has made my life worthwhile.

The first is William Shatner. (Captain J T Kirk)

I loved star trek as a child, the story gives us all hope for a positive future. William Shatner is also a very honest man. He talks about getting married at a young age, having children and feeling trapped. He openly admits he missed out on 'having fun' in his teenage years. When he met and married due to circumstance he had no idea what lay ahead. He talks about the lack of attention from the opposite sex, and the lack of guidance he was given from his closest family. He just wanted to belong to someone. Then he found fame as the buccaneering 'James T Kirk of the U.S Enterprise'. His life changed. He now had something which he did not have as a younger man, female attention. And boy did he take advantage. He lived the life of a single man even though he was married with two young children.

He is honest enough to admit, he hated himself for being so weak. He takes full responsibility for his actions. He also points out that life can be a difficult place, full of 'man traps' just waiting to get you if you have not been taught any differently.

By the age of twenty four William Shatner was famous, had money and was a divorced father of two with the world at his feet.

His first wife forgave him, as did his children, but the honesty continues when he acknowledges the fact that if he hadn't had money and status would the forgiveness been so readily there? He doubts it would.

I find this so interesting. So many people find themselves in the same position as he did, but without status. They are punished by their previous family, taunted and never forgiven. Ex-wives who fill their children with rage, never allowing their ex-partner to make amends. Making mistakes is a part of growing, not being able to put these right is unfair.

Money talks and people judge others with money.

I have always liked the way William Shatner shares his life story with openness. To bring it up to date, he did remarry twice more. His second wife died from cancer, and this affect him badly. Coping with loss has been an ever present theme throughout his life.

Now with his third wife he has realised the value of true love and devotion. One of his recent quotes was. "When you find love you need nothing else, but it must be love..."

I could not agree more.

Alison

This brings me to my wife, Alison.

The most caring, loving person I have ever had the privilege to meet. Love is the only real truth in the universe. When we discover a person who loves you for who you are no matter what, everything is possible.

My one regret is we did not meet till later in life. But then again the universe has many lessons to teach us. I'm not sure I would have learnt so much if I had met Alison any sooner.

This book and all its contents are dedicated to my best friend and wife, Alison.

Enjoyment

I hope you have enjoyed reading my experiences.

This book has written itself.

With Love,

Dominic

Endings

Coming to the end of something can leave you feeling a little deflated. A massive gap where the old routine once was. It can be hard to adjust.
I tend to want to find new things, forget about what has just been and move on fast.
But the treadmill of life will take you somewhere, whether you want to go or not. Sitting back may not be my first choice, but the calmness can focus one's mind and lead you to rediscover 'old new'.
'Old new' is all the things you used to like before you became entangled in life. Life can drag you around disorientating thoughts and passions.
I know we all change, evolve into different, but surely previous can be good?
Endings can become 'old new' starts.

Daniel Dunglass Hume

Daniel was born in Scotland in 1833, the third of eight children. His mother, Elizabeth, was a well know Scottish medium, alongside previous family members.
Daniel was a sickly baby and it is reported his cradle 'used to rock by itself' unnerving his mother.

At a year old he was passed to his childless aunt for adoption as his mother couldn't cope with him.
Along with his 'new family' Daniel emigrated at 7 years old to America. He was a nervous shy child, often playing alone; with little confidence.

Six years later he met and formed a strong bond with Edwin, and they became inseparable, talking at length and preferring walks than joining in with groups.
During their friendship they made a pact together saying that 'whoever died first' would come back and 'show themselves' to the other!

Soon after Daniel and family moved to New York and the boys lost contact, although Edwin was just 'a thought away'.

A few months after being in New York Daniel was woken by a brightly shining light at the end of the bed. As his eyes focused a vision of Edwin was within this light; whirled around and then disappeared, leaving Daniel astonished. Three days later Daniel received by letter confirmation of Edwin's death. He had contracted dysentery. Edwin, the first of the boys to pass had kept to the pact they had made.

In 1850, at seventeen years old, Daniel briefly re-united with his 'psychic' mother, Elizabeth; but was short-lived as she had predicted her own death that year and died soon after. Daniel also saw a 'vision of his mother' speaking, saying "Dan its 12 o'clock!" Which was the time of her death.

After this experience he turned to religion, becoming quite disturbed and lonely, becoming ill. Word spread around Daniel had become possessed by darker forces. Daniel started to use a power within himself to levitate and practiced on tables in his aunt's house, making lots of knocks and noises.

Locally Daniel became 'well known' for unusual happenings, but his aunt didn't want this attention so Daniel was asked to leave.

At eighteen he became known in New England and held his first séance. Still not confident and shy he found fame hard to deal with; although got fantastic reviews in newspapers on his abilities.

Two years later he took a course in medicine so he could practice, giving himself a legitimate salary, as he took no payment from séances. Unfortunately due to ongoing ill health he had to give up studying, but continued to perform, living on gifts and donations.

'Harry Houdini' attended his séances and described him as "one of the most conspicuous and lauded of his type and generation."

Everyone was convinced of Daniel Humes' credibility, although he was investigated for fraud, but no evidence was found. He continued to perform, going to Paris and The Netherlands; but did start to face public skepticism.

Daniel Hume later performed in private for just 'High Society' and handpicked guests for his audience; although always in darkened rooms.

The poet Robert Browning wasn't convinced Daniel was real and wrote a poem 'Sludge the Medium!'

In his séances he was seen with matches, a bell and oil phosphorous.

He was also supposed to have played the accordion but a mouth organ was found concealed under a very bushy moustache.

This was his life and whether people loved or loathed him he was a great entertainer.

In 1855 he held his last séance in America then contracted tuberculosis. He then came back to Europe to recuperate and didn't perform again. He said his powers were now failing and quietly faded into the background. He married into a wealthy Russian family where he converted to the Greek Orthodox Faith.

At the age of 53 in 1886 Daniel passed away from tuberculosis and is buried in a Russian cemetery.

To this day no one knows if the quiet, lonely boy from Scotland really had psychic powers or found something in life he could do well in front of adoring crowds and got the attention he so craved from performing in front of audiences worldwide.

I will let you make your own conclusions!

Alison Zenden

Guided Meditation and Visualisation.

Introduction

Everything takes preparation. The more effort you put in the better the end result.
In this first module the objective is to get you into the right frame of mind to relax long enough to clear your mind.
This might come easy to you, or you may have to work a little harder but the effort is worthwhile and please bear in mind that many fail at this stage just because they do not get the preparation right or they want instant results.
You have to train your mind to understand your five senses.
This first exercise will introduce you to this.

Useful Preparation.

Before you start your guided meditation a few useful tips:

1. Set aside a place in your home which is just for meditation. This is your special place.

2. Anything on your mind write it down before you start, you can come back to these issues later. Just release them from your mind.

3. If you have a favourite scent, fill your meditation space with it. A scent infuser is ideal. (Tea light burner.) You may need to experiment with different scents before you find the one that suits you. (Do not use naked candles, make sure you place your tea light burner in a safe place where it cannot be knocked or pushed over).

4. Never meditate tired. When you are first learning to meditate I would recommend the morning. You will find you have more control over your visualisations.

5. Make sure you have eaten, been to the toilet and have switched off any noise distractions.

This is your preparation. It will become routine and something you look forward too. (Everything involved with psychic development is a life style choice, the better you look after your body the easier the body adapts.)

Now you are ready to start.
Try not to put time limits on your first few guided meditations. With practice you will find your own timings.
You have your meditation space.
You have lit your burner.
All concerns and worries have been taken out of you mind for the time being.
(The lighting is up to you, I would recommend a dimly lit room.)

Sit at a 45 degree angle. (Try to avoid laying down.)
Breathe in to the count of 6.
Breathe out to the count of 6
Repeat this 5 times.

Feel your body relax, and gently close your eyes.

In your mind visualise a clearing in the woods.
Smell the damp grass, the scent of the trees.
Hear the birds singing, the insects buzzing.
The sun is gentle, warming your shoulders.
You start to walk towards a grand old oak tree.
You notice a door in the trunk, slightly open, with a thin crack of light shining through the gap.
This feels so inviting.
You have to open the old wooden door.
You place your hand on the cold iron door handle.
The door heavy at first, opens slowly with a squeak.
You peer inside, the scent of damp moss fills your nostrils
As your eyes get used to the light.

You can see a stone staircase which disappears as it climbs up inside the tree.

The sound of dripping water echoes as it falls on the grey stone.

Holding tight to the wooden rail you start to climb the swirly stone steps

Counting as you go.

The light at the top of the tree becomes brighter and brighter as you climb higher and higher.

Reaching the top you have counted one hundred steps.

At the top of the tree the light reveals a gap just large enough to climb through.

You duck you head, and lift your leg, first your right foot followed by your left.

As you bend your head you smell the familiar scent of a meadow.

You see the emerald green grass glinting with dew.

You hear the sound of the birds singing.

And feel the warmth of the sun on your face.

In the distance is an apple tree.

You make your way across the meadow.

Your feet damp with moisture.

As you arrive at the apple tree reach up and pick a ripe red apple.

The sweet white flesh tastes cold and crisp as you bite into the fruit.

You decide to sit down with your back up against the trunk and finish your apple.

Closing your eyes, the warm sun still on your face.

You realise you are not alone.

A white horse has come into view.

And is trotting over to meet you.

(Now it is your turn to ride bare back on the white horse, letting the animal take you wherever you want to go.

Knowing that you can return to your apple tree any time you wish.)

You can choose to meet your spirit guides or just take a look around the realm of spirit, or meet up with your loved ones who have gone before you. Your choice.

Once you are back at your apple tree just reverse the journey.

Visualise your images. Create the journey back, until you are back in the room.

Give yourself some moments to adjust. You may feel disorientated the first few times, this is normal.

With practice this meditation becomes so peaceful.

Your white horse will take you wherever you want to go.

This completes your first module. Any questions or support you need just email me.

I hope you enjoy what is a very nice way of introducing yourself to the realm of spirit.

When you have mastered this then the next stage is to understand the power of memory and how to understand thought.

Dominic j Zenden

Cracks

The Japanese have a way of thinking which I have adopted. When a piece of pottery is broken, they mend it with precious metals. The crack becomes a part of the beauty of the piece. The imperfection is not hidden, it is celebrated. A unique item. In our society we are taught to hide the cracks, the bumps and knocks. If we cannot see them, maybe they do not exist? I like imperfection, I want to be fallible. But most of all I like unique. My life is different to yours, my struggle, and my thoughts. Being broken, and fixed should be our strength, not our weakness. Never throw away something just because it was once broken.

The Front Cover

I have been seeing angels for as long as I have been working alongside spirit. I see leaf like images, multi coloured floating and swirling around the room when I connect to the realm of spirit.

I have been drawing these angels for many years.

I send my paintings all over the world. This is my way of creating awareness of how I see angels.

So what role do my personal angels fulfil? For me they help me link the two sides of life. They carry the messages from the realm of spirit and help me as a medium connect the two sides of life together.

The front cover of 'Angels on our Side' is one of over a thousand paintings I have created.

Each painting is unique. Each signed by me, and comes framed.

If you would like to buy your own unique piece of Angel Art, or enquire about the possibility of owning a piece of Angel Art designed just for you please go to my website www.myndsite.org and send me a small message.

All proceeds after expenses go to my three main charities.

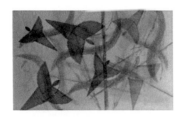

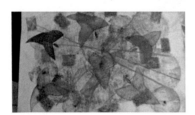

Other books by the Author:

Twitter @dominiczenden
Facebook Dominic J Zenden
E mail Auraprofiling@gmail.com
Website www.myndsite.org
Instagram - dominiczenden